Dedicated to the memory of James Benjamin "Uncle Ben" Wolf

A lover of God, people, and communities in need

The consummate community development
worker for God's Kingdom

Endorsement

"For any Christian or church globally engaged in ministering the gospel in the most intensely personal and practical of ways, this book is a must read. Jeff Palmer offers a biblical and practical way for churches and believers interested in mercy-oriented ministries to engage meaningfully and helpfully to address human needs wherever they exist in the world. With an eye toward connecting mercy-oriented ministries with evangelism, discipleship, and church planting, this book makes an invaluable contribution to sound missions practice. Far from offering a 'one size fits all' approach to meeting human needs, Jeff Palmer counsels churches to start as learners and then work with various communities in need to take ownership over solutions, all the while making the gospel a priority in every phase of ministry."

John D. Massey, PhD, dean of Roy Fish School of Evangelism and Missions, associate professor of missions

SO YOU WANT TO DIG A WELL IN AFRICA?

WHAT YOU AND YOUR CHURCH NEED TO KNOW ABOUT MERCY-ORIENTED MISSIONS

JEFF PALMER

WESTBOW
PRESS®
A DIVISION OF THOMAS NELSON
& ZONDERVAN

WestBow Press books may be ordered through booksellers or by contacting:

WestBow Press
A Division of Thomas Nelson & Zondervan
1663 Liberty Drive
Bloomington, IN 47403
www.westbowpress.com
844-714-3454

ISBN: 978-1-6642-0534-5 (sc)
ISBN: 978-1-6642-0536-9 (hc)
ISBN: 978-1-6642-0535-2 (e)

Library of Congress Control Number: 2020917603

Print information available on the last page.

WestBow Press rev. date: 10/09/2020

Contents

PART 1: TEN COMMON MYTHS (AND TRUTHS) ABOUT MERCY-ORIENTED MISSIONS

PART 2: HOW TO DEVELOP A SUCCESSFUL MERCY-ORIENTED MISSIONS PROGRAM

Foreword

I'm grateful that you are holding this book. And I hope you read it—all of it. Why? Because all of us need it.

My friendship with Jeff Palmer has been a blessing to my life, both personally and professionally. As you read this book, Jeff's expertise shines through with wise theological realities and practical implications. But there is also something else that you will see in these pages. You will see love, compassion, and respect for those on both sides of the aisle—those who "do the giving" and those who "do the receiving."

Jeff paints a picture of this mutuality for us to ponder and embrace. In a traditional sense, the givers tend to be the Western church with its access to resources. The receivers are often thought of as those who lack access to monetary resources and the benefits such resources provide. Through Palmer's lens of mutuality, however, we see that both sides have something to give each other and both sides have something to receive from each other.

But there are additional dimensions to these relationships beyond mutuality. Not only do both sides work together to transform their respective communities through discerning, dignifying, and empowering acts of compassion and mercy, they can then join forces in God's global rescue mission to the world.

As we grow in our understanding of the globalization of the missions task, Jeff paints a picture of what can be.

- A church in, say, Atlanta, wants to "dig a well in Africa."
- The Atlanta church partners with a local African church planter to do the project together.

- The well provides water for the community and launches the new church plant in that community (a double blessing for the community).
- The church in Atlanta expands not only their missions' footprint but learns valuable lessons about how mercy ministries and church starting coexist both in Africa and Atlanta.
- The church in Atlanta and the church in Africa don't stop there. This experience pushes them to keep going (hopefully in ongoing partnership with each other!) to do another community project together in a third location, maybe even among an unreached people group.

Whew. You see, our passion for compassion is often truncated. It shouldn't stop at the dug well or the newly constructed orphanage wing. God's mercy compels us to meet needs so that we can share the gospel and ultimately plant it where it does not yet exist—not only for individual people but for all the peoples of the world. Community development is a beautiful portal to God's heart for the nations.

Jeff gets this and is helping many of us get it. This book is an invaluable resource toward that end for individuals, congregations, and ministries. As a missions pastor for eighteen years, I leaned on Jeff and his expertise for effective integration of compassion and multiplication.

This approach also illustrates how mercy ministries and missions are meant to work together in a seamless fashion. Jesus modeled it for us, yet after all these years, we still tend to separate the two to the detriment of both. This book will help you recapture the fusion!

Thank you, Jeff and Regina, for helping us get it so that we can all do better and be better.

Scott Harris
Vice president of church and global engagement

Mission Increase

Introduction

MERCY-ORIENTED MISSIONS DEFINED

As you pick up this book, let me give you a spoiler alert. It is not about digging wells. It is not about Africa. So it is not about digging wells in Africa. Then what is the point of this book? And why the title? Let me explain.

Today more than ever, the world has become a smaller place. With digital connections via the internet, we can send information to the outermost corners of the world with the click of a button. We can leave home and fly almost anywhere in the world within forty-eight hours. Literally, the world is at our fingertips.

In one sense, this accessibility makes it easier to do missions. Our current generation holds great potential, ability, resources, information, and passion to help people in need around the world, and our churches are leading in this endeavor. The church is listening to its members who want to be the hands and feet of Jesus. They want to get their hands dirty doing a tangible project to help those in need. It's not just a millennial thing. More and more churches today are saying, "Let's not just give to and pray about missions; let's *do* something!"

As these churches launch cross-culturally into foreign countries, a question is continuously emerging. "Are the things we are doing actually *helping* the people we want to reach?" When we (the church) go to Africa and dig that well, does it *really* help people? The going and the digging satisfy a deep longing in our hearts. It gives us good stories to tell our friends and colleagues back home and even might give us a warm, fuzzy feeling on the inside because we've done something good. We work hard, develop a two- to three-year relationship with a person and/or a community, turn over the project (well, school, orphanage, etc.) to the people, and then move on to another missions project. But what happens when we leave? Did our project help the community in a long-term, sustainable way? Is building a well in Africa the best strategy for creating lasting, systemic change? And more importantly, is what we're doing changing lives for the gospel?

Consider this scenario: We meet someone from a different social status or even a different country. We become drawn into their story, wanting to help meet a perceived need. This compassion leads to discussion, visiting this person's home or country, and perhaps beginning long-term ministry there. We set up an organization, get a board of directors, and begin promoting the cause. Ten years down the road, we find ourselves passionately involved in and promoting a school or orphanage in country _____ (you fill in the blank). Soon the project becomes our life and ministry.

So the question is valid. Is the work we are doing really *missions?* Or is it ministry that could be done anywhere? These projects help people and make us feel good about ourselves. They also give us great adventures to share and stories to tell. We can report back to our churches with the numbers of homes we built, how many children we fed, and how many goals we accomplished on our trip. But were *missions* carried out—and were they done in a positive way?

A Conversation on an Airplane

Recently, a colleague and I took a trip to a Central American country. After boarding the plane, I noticed that we were almost the only two people who didn't have on matching T-shirts. Just about everyone else appeared to be on a mission trip. The pilot even came over the plane's intercom and thanked everyone going to this little country to help on this project. A unified cheer went up from the passengers.

A college-aged young lady sitting next to me (as well as about ten others around me) had on one of those matching shirts. I struck up a conversation that went like the following:

> Me: So you're heading down to _____ for a mission trip?
>
> Her: Well, yes, but we call it a service project.
>
> Me: Great! What are you guys going to be doing?
>
> Her: We are going to install water filters for needy communities.
>
> Me: Nice. I have done a lot of water projects in my lifetime. What kind of water filters are you installing?
>
> Her: I'm not sure. I don't know anything about water filters.
>
> Me: Hmm. Where *exactly* are you going in the country?
>
> Her: I really don't know.
>
> Me: So did you or your group leader ask the local people and community whether they need water filters?
>
> Her: Why? Everyone needs clean water, don't they?
>
> Me: Are you going to do anything else? [I was trying to lead her to a spiritual conversation.]
>
> Her: No, just water filters.

The Difference between Ministry and Missions

I want to be careful here but also ruthlessly realistic. There is a huge difference between ministry and missions. While the two can absolutely be complementary, they are two *different* things.

All followers of Jesus are called to ministry. All followers of Jesus are called to missions. However, we should not confuse the two. They are similar, interrelated, and yet very different. *Ministry is what we do to serve others.* Jesus commanded His followers, "Love the Lord your

God with all your heart, with all your soul, and with all your mind" (Matthew 22:37) and "Love your neighbor as yourself" (Matthew 22:39). Ministry is loving one's neighbor in a practical way.

More than our response to a command and simple obedience, our ministry should be a natural overflow of the Spirit of God living in us. It is the natural fruit of loving and following Jesus. It is more than something we do; it is who we are in Christ. If the apple doesn't fall far from the tree and the source of our apples is Jesus, we should minister to those around us like Jesus did.

"He went about doing good" (Acts 10:38). Jesus was moved with compassion at both the spiritual and the physical needs of people. He was consistently "teaching in their synagogues, preaching the good news of the kingdom, and healing every disease and sickness among the people" (Matthew 4:23). Our call is to minister to people in need, which reflects the heart of Jesus.

On the other hand, *missions is making the name of Christ known to the world.* It is giving God His due glory and pointing others to Him. Why? God has provided a way, the only way, for people to know Him, to have a personal relationship with Him, and to enjoy Him from now through eternity. "He made the One who did not know sin to be sin for us" (2 Corinthians 5:21) so He could offer His life as a sufficient sacrifice for the sin debt that all people owe. As simple as it sounds, our part is to accept this once-for-all sacrifice and follow Jesus by faith. The mission He then gives us is to share this good news of God's offer of grace and mercy through Jesus.

In short, missions is making disciples of all nations. God created you and me to glorify God, and we glorify God by making disciples. His desire is for all of creation to worship Him, and our role is to tell others about Him and make new worshippers called disciples. These new disciples then make more disciples and group together in new churches. These new disciples and new churches bring honor and glory to the One who rightfully deserves all glory, and they themselves become catalysts of more disciple-making and church formation unto the ends of the earth.

Here's the bottom line: Missions is not about me or you. It's not even about the people we are called to go and serve and help. It's about God. It is about God making His name known among the nations. His name will be known whether or not we participate in its proclamation, but He allows us to play a part in it.

You and I have read the Bible. We know the end of the story: God will be exalted above everything. In Philippians 2:9–11, Paul wrote,

> For this reason God highly exalted Him and gave Him the name that is above every name, so that at the name of Jesus every knee will bow—in heaven and on earth and under the earth—and every tongue will confess that Jesus Christ is Lord, to the glory of God the Father.

The remarkable thing is God has invited you and me to participate in His mission to make Himself and His Son Jesus known to a lost, needy, and dying world. *Ministry is what we do to serve others. Missions is making Christ known to unreached people and places.*

When we combine ministry with a missions focus, the result can become something greater than what those two accomplish separately. We can focus our efforts on making Christ known (missions) through word (proclamation or testimony about Jesus) and deed (ministry).

We can do ministry without doing missions. If we do not intentionally share the gospel while we are doing our work, that work can be considered an act of kindness or a good deed—ministry at its basic level. While there is nothing inherently wrong with doing good, such work by itself does not qualify as missions.

For instance, we could go dig a well in Africa, as the title of this book suggests. We could work with a community, help them get water for their village, celebrate together the success of the project, and then pack our bags and head home to America without ever sharing Christ. It is a good ministry, but it is not missions work because we have not taken the time to talk specifically about God's plan of redemption through Jesus.

Personally, I have helped many impoverished communities around the world start small-scale goat projects to help with hunger and poverty alleviation. Those "goat projects" have truly helped numerous people and communities. They have improved nutrition, increased family income, and given my organization access to countless unsaved people and communities. But there is one thing that is undeniably true: a goat cannot share the gospel.

Unless we find a way to share the gospel vocally, our projects are good deeds and good ministries. This is not bad, but it is not missions in its truest sense.

To Your Neighbor and to the Nations

Many years ago, my wife and I applied with a missions agency to serve as cross-cultural workers overseas. The agency asked about our gifts, training, and ability to share our faith. We proudly communicated our passion to share Christ and were eager to get to our first assignment so we could do just that. I still remember the next statement. "So tell me about a recent witnessing opportunity you were involved in here in the US." The point the committee was trying to make was simple. If you are aren't sharing your faith in your own country, how can you ensure that you will do so once you get overseas?

Here's the point: If you (or your church) are thinking about going overseas to do a missions or ministry project, my first question is "What missions or ministry are you doing in your own community?" If you and I are passionate about going around the world to feed the hungry, clothe the naked, respond to disasters, take care of the poor, and make Christ known, then what evidence in our lives and in our churches proves that we are committed to this passion at home as well?

The Gradient Scale: From Ministry to Mission

Recently, I had a conversation with a friend who is a missions pastor at a large church. We discussed his struggle concerning all the ministry projects their church members have done. While these would be considered good *ministry*, every one of the people doing these projects wanted to call the them *mission* projects because they took place outside the walls of the church. I believe many other church leaders wrestle with this same problem.

My friend and I decided there were several levels of ministry/ mission projects. Some are pure ministry, meaning they demonstrate love for God but are not focused on the proclamation of the gospel, a defining characteristic of missions. Other projects emphasize witnessing as the primary goal. This distinction is important to him as a missions pastor because he is constantly bombarded with requests for resources for ministry and/or missions projects in the US and all over the world. Since these requests come from church members, he struggled to determine which ones the church should support and the appropriate amount of support to give.

When we talked about assigning levels to these projects in terms of a ministry versus missions focus, we began to see a pattern that would give some structure to evaluating which projects to support as ministry and which to support as missions. Some proposed projects would not meet the criteria for either.

Level 1: Ministry Only

Some ministry projects focus solely on actions to meet current, physical needs (feed orphans, provide health care services, supply clean water, etc.). These good deeds are done in the name of Christ. Some people might come to a saving faith in Christ through the project and those who share their faith as they work. These projects focus on ministering to people in need, but there is little or no strategy for intentionally sharing Christ or making disciples other than what occurs organically. The beneficiaries of this approach are generally limited to the target group or organization (a school, clinic, orphanage, etc.). Think of, for example, a well drilling/water development team that goes into a community to help them have clean drinking water. The team is effective and efficient at what it does (getting clean water to the community) but doesn't utilize their time and opportunities to share the gospel and make disciples feeling that "clean water" in itself is a good work that bears witness in and of its own self.

Level 2: Ministry with Some Evangelism and Discipleship

These ministry projects are similar to those in level 1, but with an added emphasis on evangelism and discipleship. Participants in these trips undergo training with the expectation and accountability to share their faith and disciple new believers as they go about the ministry project. Again, think of that same well-drilling team. Maybe one or two strong evangelists on the team share the gospel while others in the group drill the well. In this case, gospel presentation is limited and there is little or no follow-up to see emerging local believers grouped into a local church.

Level 3: Ministry with a Church-Planting Focus

These projects focus not only evangelism and discipleship strategy but also on small group formation in the community where ministry is taking place. In other words, these ministry/mission projects intentionally lead to the formation or planting of a church. Again, think of the well project as an example. Typically, the well drillers would live in and be involved with the community during the four to six weeks necessary to complete the water system. They use their time wisely and share their faith during both work and rest hours. They see a few individuals become believers and start a small church in the area before leaving. This approach produces good results, but the church planting is driven by the outsiders, not the new Christians.

Level 4: Ministry Empowering Local Believers

Ministry projects at this level incorporate the strategies of prior levels but with an added strategy of empowering local believers and their churches. This takes place through training, discipling, and outreach to their neighbors and communities. Local believers offer the same compassion they have received, but with an intentional gospel witness. Again, take the well drilling example, but in this case, the water development team is a highly trained and equipped group of *local* believers. They share their faith and start a new church in the community where they are working. They also give continuous, long-term attention to the growth and empowerment of that local church so it can then become a reproducing church in other communities.

Level 5: Ministry with a Missions Focus

These projects meet the needs of the target population and create access to unreached and unengaged peoples for the express purpose of sharing the gospel. First and foremost, these projects focus on telling others about Jesus but utilize ministry projects as the tool that opens the door to these conversations. Once again, think of a locally staffed water development team that sees their water ministry as a missional strategy. They utilize their well-drilling skills to gain access to areas previously unreached by believers. They evangelize, disciple, and intentionally form churches as they go. They also seek to help those churches reproduce themselves and move on to other areas that need clean water and access to the gospel.

All of these levels of ministry projects are valid. Which one you (or your group) gravitate toward will depend largely on your calling, gifting, and vision. However, as you move down these levels, you move toward a truer *missions* emphasis. If the goal of a church and/or a believer is to make His name known to those who have never heard it, that church needs to focus its time and resources on projects at levels 4 and 5.

Bringing the Idea Home

For a couple of years, I have hesitated to write this book. Having lived and worked overseas doing holistic missions for over twenty years, I felt a bit out of touch with churches in the US and the changes going on within them. I was comfortable using agriculture, health care, water, literacy, and similar ministries to engage the unreached of the world and to train others to utilize the principles and skills I had learned. I also had positive experiences directing volunteers who had come on mission trips to help my team and me in our work.

When I returned to the US a few years ago and became reacquainted with my home church and its people, I realized that the approach churches and individuals took to get involved in missions had changed radically. To better understand this seismic shift, I took a few years to learn more by visiting, training, and working with several churches.

This book comes out of my experiences overseas and in the US. It will try to address the common questions and problems I hear everywhere I go. These concerns come from churches and individuals who have gone out, tried to do some type of ministry project, such as dig a well, host a health care clinic, or build a training center, and still wonder whether or not their work was effective.

The stories I use to illustrate my points (especially those at the beginning of each chapter) are not intended to single out or ridicule any one person or missions group. They are based on actual conversations and experiences from *multiple* encounters with people. Most of the encounters have happened more than once. In other words, they are common obstacles and questions I hear from church members interested in doing mission ministry projects. I won't pretend to have *all* the answers, but I will try to provide *some* answers and suggestions that have worked in my experience.

I hope this book will stimulate good conversations between your fellow church members and you. I also hope it will spur discussion about efficient and effective ways to minister to people around the world and make Christ's name known in the process.

The structure of the book is laid out logically (in my mind). The first section defines and introduces the concept of mercy-oriented missions. The second section addresses ten common myths and misperceptions I hear from people and churches who want to do missions projects. The third section provides strategy and tools to assist an individual or organization already involved in or wanting to implement a missions strategy. It also highlights the mercy of God in the ministry of Jesus and how this applies to our overall missions calling and effort. The book concludes with references and resources for further exploration on this topic.

I pray your journey in reading this book will be a fruitful one. I hope it will challenge you to assess, evaluate, and possibly adjust some of the ways you carry out your mission programs. I believe the lessons and tools within these pages can equip you to do missions more effectively in your local and global outreach for God and for His glory.

> We proclaim Him, warning and teaching everyone with all wisdom, so that we may present everyone mature in Christ. I labor for this, striving with His strength that works powerfully in me. (Colossians 1:28–29)

PART 1

TEN COMMON MYTHS (AND TRUTHS) ABOUT MERCY-ORIENTED MISSIONS

MYTH: "THE LOCAL PEOPLE HAVE NOTHING!"

(TRUTH: EVEN POOR PEOPLE HAVE RESOURCES.)

So God created man in His own image; He created him in the image of God; He created them male and female.

—Genesis 1:27

Recently, a local church asked me to visit with its missions committee and teams. For several years, the church had taken trips to a country to build churches, conduct vacation Bible schools, and help with some water projects. Church members had been moved by the perceived poverty of the local population (of both believers and nonbelievers) and wanted to help them.

Like I commonly do, I asked the committee to describe a typical local community they worked with every year. They identified three geographical areas where they worked but the descriptions always included the statement "The local people have nothing!"

This thought ran through my mind: *The local people have nothing? Really?* I said a quick, silent prayer for wisdom. Then I resumed by asking a couple of simple questions.

1

Me: So the local people have nothing?

Missions Committee: Absolutely nothing.

Me: So they don't have clothes?

Missions Committee: Don't be absurd. Of course they have clothes, but they are basically rags unfit for anyone to wear.

Me: So they don't have houses?

Missions Committee: Of course they have houses, but they are small, poorly constructed, and consist of only one or two rooms.

Me: I don't know this place well, but don't the people there have great community celebrations such as *fiestas*, weddings, and gatherings and special events like funerals? Can you describe those?

Missions Committee: Yes! We've been there when the town hosts a *fiesta*. It is amazing. They invite other villages in to celebrate, and the celebration goes on for days. There is food, dancing, and singing. It's something to see. We have also been there during weddings and other celebrations. They really know how to throw an event!

Me: So who pays for these events? Where do they get the money for their *fiestas*, weddings, and other celebrations?

Missions Committee (after pausing): Well, I guess the people do.

Me: But I thought you said they had nothing.

Missions Committee (becoming a bit uncomfortable): They don't! You have never seen poverty like this!

Me: Hmm …

How We View Poverty Affects How We Treat People in Need

How we perceive someone determines how we interact with them. For instance, if we see a beggar along a highway off-ramp in the US, we might perceive this person as a bum who needs to get cleaned up and get a job. This might lead us to look the other way or glare at them in pity or anger, assuming they could do better. However, if we saw this person and believed they were on the down and out, a victim of circumstances, and in need of a helping hand, we might stop, roll down our window, and give them something.

The truth is we can't know the why and what of a person's condition by looking at them through a car windshield, can we? As a default, we react (or not) to a person based on our preconceived judgments. Our thoughts and ideas about a person also depend on our mood or feelings at that moment. We could be in a hurry and use that as an acceptable excuse to look the other way. We could be so distracted by a crying child in the backseat that we don't even see the beggar by the road. We could be dealing with a stressful situation. Or we could have had a bad experience with a beggar that would cause negative feeling toward the current person we see (whom we don't even know). Common reactions to beggars might be the following:

- I can ignore them. They are professional con artists exploiting me.
- I can roll down the window and lecture them. Anybody can get a job, can't they?
- I can smile and wave at them and maybe tell them to have a nice day. I might even shout to them and say I will pray for them.
- I can reach into my pockets or console in my car, looking for a small amount of money (or something else) to give them. It helps alleviate my guilt.
- _____ (Insert your response here. There are more than I can name.)

None of the above reactions is helpful for one main reason: they don't take into account how the person ended up on the side of the road asking for money. However, to stop and talk with them takes time, which most of us are not willing to give. Stopping also puts us in an uncomfortable place: in a relationship with a person in need. How many of us would be willing to develop a relationship with someone begging on the side of the road? Not many.

I will be the first to admit I do not stop to help everyone I see in need. In fact, I probably stop and help less than I should. I am often moved with compassion but not enough compassion to act on a person's behalf. I grieve the Holy Spirit because I see a need and am prompted to stop and interact with that person, but because of a legion of excuses, I choose to walk or drive past them, often with these thoughts and emotions running through my head:

- I'm busy and don't have time!
- I can't meet all the needs of the world, can I?
- I'm afraid because if I stop and take time, I don't know where this will lead. After all, that person is probably suffering from a mental illness, right?

While these emotions and reasons could contain a nugget of truth in them, those lines of reasoning devolve into a set of excuses I use to convince myself I shouldn't get involved.

Jesus Stopped When He Saw People in Need

When I look at the life and ministry of Jesus, I see something completely different. True, He didn't meet every need presented to Him. At times He withdrew from the pressing needs of the crowds. He could have been fatigued. He could have been guarding against people following Him for what He could do for them. He could have had a number of other reasons for choosing not to meet a need.

However, it is important to pay attention to the number of times

Jesus heard the cry of someone in need, took the time to stop and interact with them, and touched them in the areas of their deepest needs.

The healing of the two blind men (Matthew 20:29–34). As Jesus was leaving Jericho to go to Jerusalem (and the cross), two blind men sitting by the roadside called out, "Lord, have mercy on us, Son of David!" (v. 30). The crowd tried to shush the blind men. They wanted to hear Jesus. However, Jesus heard the men's cries, stopped walking, and called them closer. And even more amazing, Jesus asked them, "What do you want Me to do for you?" (v. 32). Even though He was traveling to the cross, Jesus still had the sensitivity to hear the cry of two people in need, had the patience to stop and talk to them, and had the compassion to ask the men what they needed. When they answered, "Lord ... open our eyes" (v. 33), Matthew recorded, "Moved with compassion, Jesus touched their eyes. Immediately they could see, and the followed him" (v. 34).

The healing of a leper (Matthew 8:1–4). After the Sermon on the Mount (Matthew 5–7), Jesus came down from the mountain with great crowds following Him. In the midst of the masses, an unclean and socially outcast leper came to Him, knelt before Him, and said, "Lord, if you are willing, you can make me clean" (v. 2). At this, Jesus did the unthinkable—at least to the crowds who had attended his mountainside revival services. Jesus stopped, reached out his hand, touched the leper (possibly touching the most disfigured part of his body), and said, "I am willing; be made clean" (v. 3). Mark's gospel account tells us that Jesus was "moved with compassion" when he healed this man (Mark 1:41).

The encounter with a Samaritan woman (John 4:1–26). In John's gospel, we read the account of Jesus's interaction with a Samaritan woman at a public well. Jesus, weary from his journey, was sitting beside the well when the woman from Samaria came to draw water (John 4:6). Jesus engaged her in a conversation that started with a simple request. "Give Me a drink" (v. 7). This led to a deep conversation regarding her life, her failures, and the hope she could have in the Savior of the world—the Living Water. The woman was in need emotionally and spiritually, and Jesus met her at her deepest level of need. He was tired. He was thirsty. His earthly nation (Israel) was not even on speaking terms with the woman's people (Samaritans). But He stopped, took time, spoke to her, and cared for her where she needed it the most.

In all the above cases (and more), Jesus fully understood what the people needed—even before they spoke to Him. He was, after all, the Savior of the world, the second person of the Trinity, and cocreator and sustainer of the universe. Pretty impressive credentials. But in each case, He stopped and took time for the individual. He gave those in need the dignity to express what they were seeking. He offered a solution to their needs that also required faith on their part.

These gospel encounters provide some basic principles to help us when confronted by needs of individuals as well as the masses.

1. We are not called to meet every need. One of the beautiful things about Jesus that we see in the New Testament is that there is no example of anyone who came to Him in faith with a need that He didn't heal. However, I assume that Jesus didn't meet every need of every person He passed by. In the crowds that followed Jesus and the multitudes He passed by, surely there were sick and needy people whom Jesus did not heal. Maybe it's because they didn't cry out in faith. Maybe it's because of some unknown reason to us. However, if true, this would show us that the responsibility of meeting every need and solving every problem doesn't have to fall on our shoulders.

2. We should look at our encounters with people through the eyes of Jesus. While I am not called to meet *every* need, more often than not I pass up divine opportunities because of my own selfish interests and agendas. Jesus saw His interactions with people as a chance to engage them and give them hope.

3. We should follow Jesus's example. We should be willing to stop, ask questions, listen to people's stories, and act in a way that truly helps them and brings glory to God. It is easier (and thus tempting) to put a Band-Aid on a problem rather than find a real solution. The Band-Aid allows me to do *something*, feel good about meeting a moral obligation, and move on to my next exciting and challenging adventure. Finding a long-term solution requires a lot more time, preparation, investment, and resources. And honestly, to take the time would slow me down and derail my person agenda. Taking time to understand or get involved in someone's complicated need is scary. What will be required of me? What will I have to give up? What are the risks? I'm not always comfortable with the investment needed to adequately address the problem at hand.

Remember Everyone Can Give Something

People have an amazing capacity to survive, thrive, create, and grow. Some are at a disadvantage resource-wise. They may not have the assets we have to start a small business or increase their food production. They may not have the formal education we enjoy. They may have limited access to knowledge-based tools we take for granted, like simple internet research. They may not have a nice retirement fund to fall back on in their sixties so they can enjoy the "good life." They may have lost everything to a natural disaster. Or in many cases, they may face a problem like armed conflict, corruption-induced poverty, or human trafficking. However, in most every case, they have *something* to give.

- They have skills and local knowledge.
- They can do manual labor (in most cases).
- They have some material resources.
- Many exhibit a self-determination unrivaled by anything we bring to the table.
- They have a brain and creativity because, like you and me, they are created in God's image.

Story of a West African Village

A few years back, I was privileged to work with some local teams in West Africa conducting community development workshops. I shared the principle of communities taking ownership of their problems as well as the solutions to those problems. And ideally, the community would solve their identified needs largely through local knowledge and resources already available to them. Sounds easy, right?

The group was skeptical to the idea. The villages where they worked were populated by poor, semi-nomadic peoples who were used to outsiders coming into their communities with "solutions" to their problems (in the form of handouts). In the group's opinion, the local people were lazy, corrupt, and manipulative. You couldn't trust them one bit. At this point, I was beginning to question whether or not we had chosen the right teams or the right place to begin a community development program.

For a few days, we trained and learned together the basics of community development, practicing some of the tools for interacting with a community. We stressed, as we always do, that development must originate from the insiders in the community. It needs to be participatory, facilitate a sustainable solution using the community's resources, and ultimately lead toward transformation of individuals and the community as a whole. When it came time to visit a village and practice some of the things we learned, the doubts of the participants had only increased.

After several hours of driving on a dusty, bumpy road, our small group arrived at the designated community. Led by their chief dressed in local attire, the whole community greeted us like royalty. After appropriate introductions and accompanying refreshments, we began to share with the community and its leaders the purpose of our visit. We wanted to learn about their community, their challenges, as well as their resources.

The chief spoke for the entire community. He began by telling us how poor they were. They didn't have a good school. Life was hard. The roads were bad. They needed help building a clinic because the only access to health care services was far away. The list of needs went on and on. I glanced at the faces of my companions, and it was almost as if they said, "See? We told you so."

At the appropriate time, I began to interject questions. I asked him to name the positive aspects about the community. It had existed for more than a hundred years, so there had to be reasons it still remained. What were some of the things they liked about the area? Why did they stay?

I mentioned how their land looked fertile, at least the part I saw as we drove in. The chief replied, "Yes, we have some of the best land in all of our country." I also asked about the herds of animals we saw nearby. Again, the chief replied, "Yes, we have some of the best goats and sheep in all of this area." Then I mentioned the large river that flowed close by, and again the chief replied, "Yes, we have an abundance of water—some of the best anywhere!" Before long, we heard all the good things about the community and the amazing resources that brought them pride.

With mutual respect, we entered a development process with this community, which eventually led to building a local health center. We as the outsiders helped, but the people did most of the work and provided a large portion of the resources needed to construct and manage the small clinic.

If we only look on the surface and evaluate others from our experiences and biases, we will not see the resources people have at hand. Even the poorest of the poor can offer something. Yes, they have many needs, but they also have an amazing ability to address those needs. Sometimes they need help from the outside. But in many cases, with a little bit of time and effort, they can find amazing solutions themselves. Best of all, if the solutions and the majority of the resources come from within the community, there will be a greater chance that those solutions will be sustainable. Simply put, an area's development doesn't need to be dependent on outsiders' help.

What We Learned

- We can discover what others can give (time, resources, skills, etc.) if we stop and take time to learn and understand.
- We need to look at people from Jesus's perspective, rather than relying on our own cultural myths and biases.
- Most everyone has something to give.

MYTH: "THE PEOPLE WE WORK WITH ARE HELPLESS!"

(TRUTH: HOW WE SEE POVERTY AFFECTS HOW WE TREAT PEOPLE IN NEED.)

What is a human being that You remember him, a son of man that You look after him? You made him a little less than God and crowned him with glory and honor. You made him ruler over the works of Your hands; You put everything under his feet.

—Psalm 8:4–6

I sat across the desk from a local minister of missions. He was struggling with a request to support the newly proposed missions project idea of one of his church members. It really wasn't a good project, and the person proposing the missions project was not the best qualified and equipped to take on such a project. To make things a bit more awkward, the person proposing the project was sitting in the room.

> Missions Pastor: Well, Bill, I don't know that we can support your idea.

Bill: *What do you mean?* I've been a faithful member [of this church] and I truly believe God is telling me to do this. If you don't get behind me on this, I feel that you are standing in the way of God's will.

Missions Pastor (sheepishly, to me): What do you think, Jeff?

Me (a bit hesitant since I'm the outsider in the room and have been thrown into the middle of this discussion): Well, it seems Bill is passionate about this project, and he believes God is leading him to do it. However, I tend to agree with you [the missions pastor] that this is not a good idea from a missions' perspective.

Bill (growing agitated): But you don't understand! We *have* to do this project, and we have to do it *this* way. The people there [referring to the place he had visited overseas] are pretty much helpless. They can't do anything right. They don't know how to do anything by modern methods.

Me: Hmmm …

The Smartest Person in the World

One of my mentors of ministry missions is the late Dr. Warlito "Wal" Laquihon. Wal and his wife, Ellen, took Regina, my wife, and me under their wings when we first went to the Philippines. Along with several other Western missionaries and Filipino believers, this couple gave us a wealth of insight about cross-cultural mercy-oriented missions, local language and culture, and in many cases, ourselves and our shortcomings. Wal used to say that the poor Filipino farmer is the smartest person in the world. It took me several years of working with these farmers to understand what Dr. Laquihon was trying to teach me.

Regina and I went to the Philippines in the early 1980s armed with the latest and greatest training, education, and ideas in both agriculture and health care. I had grown up "hobby" farming in rural Tennessee and had a new, shiny master's degree in agriculture from a state university. Regina had her nursing degree and a year's experience working in a modern county hospital. We were going to show rural, poor Filipinos how to farm and how to be healthy.

It wasn't long until we realized what Dr. Laquihon and others had come to understand. We were going to "help" people who obviously had fewer resources than we did, such as material goods, formal education, and a salary complete with benefits. However, these people we were trying to help were by no means helpless.

The average community of rural/tribal Filipinos where we worked had anywhere from thirty to one hundred families living in that community. Most families farmed for a living and derived their livelihood from their farming activities. They were "upland" farmers, meaning they lived on gentle slopes. However, in many cases, they lived on mountainsides with very steep slopes.

The average farm family lived on two or three acres of land. They grew corn as their staple food. They ground it and cook the "grits" like you'd cook rice. It provided energy in their diet. They grew vegetables and raised a few animals (free-range chickens, goats, maybe a pig). They also hunted, fished, and gathered wild plants and nuts if they were fortunate to live close to a forest or body of water. It wasn't uncommon for members of a family to maintain a small side business, such as sewing or chopping firewood. This work would supplement the family income. It was also common for older family members to seek day labor to enhance the family income.

In good years, a typical farming family could grow enough corn and other agricultural products to feed the family and still have surplus to sell for much-needed cash. In bad years, they lacked enough food to eat and went long periods with nothing to sell. As a result, they couldn't purchase necessities like soap, toothpaste, school supplies, and other items.

The average house was about sixteen feet by twenty feet in size. It had wood frames, bamboo sides, and a grass roof (or a tin roof if the family had more money). The house usually consisted of two rooms:

a sitting area (often with earthen floor) and a usually raised area for the family to sleep. A family consisting of father, mother, and three or four children would live in this house together.

Here's why the poor, rural Filipino farmer is the smartest person in the world: They are able to raise, feed, clothe, educate, house, and provide for their family of five or six while living on a small parcel of land they farmed. At best, they would make $15 to $25 a month (US currency) over and above their consumption needs, which were met mostly from the produce of their farm. They could do all of this by using only very basic resources.

When Wal would tell this story, he would ask the listener this question: "Could you do the same?" In other words, if you and I were given the same resources and challenges, could we survive like that "poor" Filipino farmer? Or would we give up after a few days or weeks, destined to starve?

Wal would say the Filipino farmer is the best agriculturist: he can feed his family with little land. He would also say the Filipino farmer is one of the world's best economists. He could provide for his family's needs with little or no money. So there's the proof: the poor Filipino farmer is the smartest man in the world!

People Are Not Helpless

It takes a while for Americans to realize that people with fewer resources than us still have unique abilities. Wherever you go and whatever people you find, that population is already developing at its own pace, unless it is under some type of natural or man-made disaster event. That development and progress may not look like what happens in the US. In a few cases, it is actually *better*. In poorer societies, the development or progress can be negligible, hidden, or even undetectable due to our cultural biases and filters. But it is still developing.

A Westerner walking into an urban slum in Kenya for the first time has no framework to interpret what they are seeing, smelling, hearing, and experiencing. Naturally, they would filter everything attacking their senses through their comfortable suburban America lifestyle, culture, and experience. This is not bad. It's just our frame of reference. We all see and interpret things based on our knowledge and experiences.

The Westerner introduced to a Kenyan slum would probably see inadequate housing—shanties made of tin, cardboard, and other materials—stacked side by side and, in some cases, on top of one another. They would smell and see the piles of rotting garbage and might even detect a whiff of open sewage. A lot of people, mainly women and children, would be sitting in small groups outside the shanties in whatever bit of shade they could find. Dirt and filth would be everywhere, and it would be safe to conclude (from the Westerner's perspective) that no one should live in these conditions. The outsiders would sense a strong urge to do something about it—to go on a crusade to clean up the place, to educate the residents, and for heaven's sake, to make those "houses" more livable!

However, if a local person from that country walked into the same community, they would see something totally different because they come from the same culture and background. They might see housing for people who may not have any other place to go, so the shanties are actually pretty nice. They might also see that although there are piles of garbage and refuse around the neighborhood, the areas near the front door and inside the shanties are swept clean every day and kept neat. That local person might know that those groups of ladies sitting together are close friends talking, laughing, and fellowshipping because it's the middle of the day and they have already been working eight hours. This is their favorite part of the day—when they can sit and visit with family and friends. They might also see happy people who don't have a lot of possessions but who have a lot of friends and a great community. And they would probably see lots of industry and productivity, but not the kind the Western visitor would have seen as they looked at the same community.

Same community, different eyes and different lenses seeing that community.

Lessons I've Learned from Working with the Poor

As a young missionary who utilized community development, I thought I would be the teacher. At times, I could make a contribution in the area of food production, or I could help a family raise their animals better to improve their livelihood. However, I discovered quickly that I was the one who learned the most. The "teacher" became the student.

Here are a few things I learned—mostly the hard way. To be frank, I am still learning these lessons today.

1. The "poor" are people. Removing labels from people would serve us well. "Poor" *seems* like a benign word we use to describe those with fewer resources than we enjoy. In reality, it is a pejorative term that automatically labels a person or community and puts them into a subservient class or category in our minds, whether we realize it or not. Without meaning to do so, the term sets us up as "the haves" and the poor as "the have nots." The "poor" are real people, and we must see them as such. People with problems but people with joys. People with struggles but people who love their families, work, and lives. People with limited resources but people with amazing capacities and abilities.

2. The "poor" have amazing capabilities to solve a lot of their problems if given the chance. I have witnessed the poorest of the poor in the world (as an outsider would classify them) accomplish remarkable things. I think about the women's groups in one South Asian country. Over 150 community groups have formed, comprising about twenty to thirty women per group. They meet once per week to discuss their problems, encourage one another, and place the equivalent of twenty-five US cents into a community kitty used to fund projects approved by the group members. These self-help groups are now funding poverty alleviation projects, such as animal distribution, seed dispersal, start-up capital for small businesses, and many others. After four years, these 4,000 women in total now hold assets of close to US $70,000! All of this is their money from *their* resources and savings!

3. The "poor" and poor communities understand their communities—the positives and negatives—better than any outsiders would. They have lived there for generations. They have lived in the good times and bad. They know the relationships. They also know what has and hasn't worked.

When I as an outsider come to their community, they politely receive me and listen to my ideas and thoughts because of their cultural values of honoring visitors. To avoid shaming me, community leaders will listen to my ideas and even support them because not to would be rude and I (the outsider) might lose face. They will even go along with any programs or plans that I might propose to the community because it is polite to do so. And who knows? It might bring some benefit to the community.

However, whatever is introduced from the outside generally won't be widely adopted or sustained. Life is fragile when you live in poverty with limited resources and options. And what they have been doing for decades has worked. They have survived. Remember if you and I were dropped into their situations with their resources, we probably would be dead within a month! They might not be "blowing and growing" in their development, but they are surviving and thriving, even if not to our Western standards.

4. I have a lot of fears, misperceptions, and cultural biases to overcome as I work with the "poor." Once I was in the home of a young man (who looked very old) dying with AIDS. He had been the bread winner of the family, so now the family was impoverished not only because of loss of his income but also because of the expense to keep him alive. His wife couldn't work. Someone had to be his caregiver and watch their children.

A case worker and I delivered some goods to his family and him, and I asked if I could pray with him. He smiled weakly, said yes, and reached out his bony hand so I could hold it as we prayed. I froze. It was only for a second, but I was ashamed. Here he lay dying and all he asked for was the comfort of a simple touch and prayer, yet I froze. In my mind, I knew there was little to no chance of his transmitting the disease to me through a hand clasp. But my fear and cultural bias welled up and formed a huge ball in my throat. I did take his hand and pray, but I was reminded of my sin-filled filters once again.

5. God is honored by our efforts to help those in need. I've often said that there is a special place in the heart of God for the poor, needy, and downtrodden. Throughout the Bible, He advocates for the widow, the orphan, and the stranger. Of course, God loves everyone and doesn't want any to perish. He wants all people to come to repentance and a right relationship with Him (2 Peter 3:9). But in Luke's gospel, Jesus said, "Blessed are you who are poor, because the kingdom of God is yours" (Luke 6:20). I am constantly amazed at the spirituality of the poor worldwide. They value relationships (for the most part) and tend to be more relational and interdependent than those with more resources. I believe a part of their reasoning is that when you have little to depend on, you always have God and your neighbors. Sometimes my resources get in the way of my need for God.

Bringing It Home

The Bible warns believers against viewing the poor and seemingly weaker person as less valuable than those who have money (James 2:1–9). It also tells us to be careful about how we treat the poor (Proverbs 14:31) and cautions us, "Do not be partial to the poor or give preference to the rich" (Leviticus 19:15).

God values all people. As believers, our view and treatment of people should be rooted in the heart of God. People are the penultimate crown of His creation. God provided a way of salvation and eternal fellowship between humans and Himself. We are the only part of creation given this honor. Even angels marvel at this fact (1 Peter 1:10–12).

When we work with people in mercy-oriented mission projects and strategies, we should not treat them as poor, helpless, unresourceful, or _____ (you add the adjective). They are people created in the image of God, with real physical needs and a great eternal need to be reconciled to their Maker. In truth, they are just like me and you, only with fewer earthly resources.

What We Learned

- People are not helpless. On the contrary, they are amazingly resourceful.
- We have a lot to learn from those we work with.
- When we work with those we deem "poor," we have to overcome the bias steeped in our own lives.
- God values all people.

MYTH: "ALL THEY HAVE TO EAT ARE RICE AND BEANS!"

(TRUTH: PEOPLE HAVE A REASON FOR WHAT THEY DO.)

There is an occasion for everything, and a time for every activity under heaven.

—Ecclesiastes 3:1

I was meeting with a missions team getting ready to head overseas. They were going back to a familiar area where they had seen firsthand the poverty and needs of the people. They described the situation to me. Having lived overseas while working with rural communities for twenty years, what I heard didn't seem particularly bad. I mentioned that the poverty and hunger they had seen and described weren't life-threatening. In fact, they were normal for a developing country.

I had crossed a line.

One of the team members stood up, pointed her finger at me, and with a reddened face said, "You don't understand how poor these people are. All they have to eat are rice and beans!"

I paused because I realized I had hit a nerve. I took a deep breath, said a quick prayer for wisdom, and asked a question. "So how long have they been eating rice and beans?"

"For hundreds of years!" The red-faced lady was becoming more agitated.

Again I paused and prayed for wisdom. I didn't know how to proceed. At that moment, another team member spoke up. "You know, I think they *like* to eat rice and beans." To my relief, the majority of the group agreed and pointed out the nutritional value of rice and beans.

People Generally Have a Reason for Doing the Things They Do

I know this statement sounds simplistic, but it's true: people have a reason for doing what they do. The problem is we make hasty judgments before we stop to understand the reason behind their actions (or inactions). What we see as a priority may not be as important to someone else.

As an outsider, it is tempting to walk into a community and immediately identify the problems needing correction in order to make it a better place. It's easy to see the need for a better water system, more passable roads, better farming techniques, improved animal breeds, etc. I know the temptation because I've been guilty of it.

I remember one particular village I visited. The hunger was obvious. Even without quantifiable measurements, I could tell the children were undernourished. When we looked at their potential food production, I noticed they planted their food crops far away from their homes. To make things more confusing, they farmed on highly sloping land, which meant it was fragile—subject to erosion and not very fertile. I didn't understand why they farmed here when I could see flat, fertile land nearby. Why didn't the people farm that land?

When I brought up my brilliant solution to the community, one of its members immediately pointed out a serious flaw in my logic.

Local herds of elephants frequently tromped through the flat land in question. The shifting herds would trample anything planted there. Also, the elephants might attack a farmer in that field if they saw him as a threat. Score: Insiders: 1, Outsider: 0. I learned the importance of knowing all the facts before making suggestions.

Our role in mercy-oriented missions is to offer help where needed, not to change a community's way of life because it is antiquated or not modern enough in our estimation. Progress carries its own price, and each community needs to determine whether the change is necessary or even favorable.

What about Harmful Practices?

One community I visited used a contaminated water source because they believed an evil curse caused diseases, not polluted water. In that case, we intervened and demonstrated the water's contaminant and convinced the local leadership to find a new water source. In that situation, intervention was the right course of action. The question is "When should we as outsiders step in to offer our input and suggestions?"

Before comment about a questionable practice or custom (from an outsider's perspective), we need to assess the situation using a series of questions.

1. Is it beneficial? The first question is whether the practice or custom is safe and fair to the members of the community. Does it bring positive benefit to the people? If so, we need to leave the practice alone. Many times, we as outsiders look at a local practice or custom and do not understand its history, implications, and ramifications. Because we haven't done it that way, the temptation is to jump in and show the community a better way to do things—*our* way of doing it.

A common example is growing corn under low-production conditions. Most corn (a staple food in many areas) grown in developing countries is done in low-management, low- to medium-fertility conditions, and with open-pollinated (OPV) seeds. Better management programs (weeding and pest control), commercial fertilizer (bought from an ag-supply store), and hybridized seeds (also bought from a seed dealer) would probably generate higher yields, at least initially. This would provide more food and more potential income to the farming family. Sounds like a good idea, right?

Maybe not.

First, higher production systems cost more. These costs can place the family at a greater risk for financial ruin. For you and me who have salaries, health benefits, and retirement funds, calculated risk is not a big deal. However, for those who live on the edge of poverty and exist by subsistence farming (a huge part of the world), taking such a risk could be a matter of life and death.

Second, higher production depends mostly on the ability to procure outside inputs, such as chemical fertilizers, pesticides, and hybrid seed. Traditional open-pollinated seeds do not produce as high a yield as the hybridized seed, but they can be saved year after year. This negates the cost of buying hybrid seed each year.

Third, most open-pollinated varieties produce better than hybrids under low-fertility soil conditions. A high-production system utilizing chemicals and hybrid seed on fragile soils can rapidly lead to nutrient depletion. This depletion can render local soils and environments unproductive within two to three years. This is *very* risky for the poor farmer.

In a situation like this, if the local custom or practice is working and is beneficial, we as outsiders need to leave it alone at least until we have time to understand why the practice still exists.

2. Is it neutral? In other words, is the practice neither beneficial nor harmful, as far as you can tell? If so, you and I need to let it go for now. Let the people address the issue or need when they see a problem with it, and look for more pressing needs.

One of the communities I worked in had already established a water system by the time we entered their area. It was a free-flowing spring water system, but it had been constructed poorly and inefficiently. They had closed-off a mountain spring about a mile away from their community. It was at a significantly higher elevation, so they ran plastic (polyurethane) pipes from the spring down to the village. When the pipe fed into the community, the people cut random notches in the tube to access the water, which wasted a lot of water and created some big mud holes in the communal areas. We could have shown them how to make a simple catchment reservoir to store the water in volumes, benefiting the whole community. It would create cleaner and nicer conditions too. However, the people didn't see the need. The water was plentiful, so they preferred to concentrate on other problems they perceived as more important. Eventually, the community did address the messy, inefficient system, but only when it was ready to do so.

The poorly constructed water system worried me more than it worried the community. I had to learn—and I am still learning—to let these things go. No harm, no foul!

3. Is it harmful or life-threatening? Could the local practice bring harm to people? If so, we need to intervene with an alternative.

For instance, some local health care practices can make sick people worse or even become the cause of death. In rural Southeast Asia as in many parts of the world, the people once believed the best way to treat a fever was to wrap the person up because they appeared to be cold and were shivering. Caregivers wanted to keep the warmth inside the body and keep the bad air out, because evil spirits resided in bad air. Of course, this cocooning practice traps the heat in and can cause the body temperature to spike even higher. If continued, this practice can cause heat exhaustion, dehydration, convulsions, and even death.

In these same rural areas of the world, the local people stop giving fluids to someone with diarrhea (a common ailment in those places) or vomiting. The rationale is the vomiting and diarrhea will stop if the sick person is not given fluids. This may be true, but the patient will become dehydrated, which can lead to death if not treated.

In these situations, we as outsiders need to step in and offer solutions. This can take the form of education or even direct intervention. However, best processes call for us to evaluate an "odd" custom or behavior (from our perspective) before running in with a solution. If the practice is not harmful, if it is beneficial or even neutral, then we leave the people to continue that practice, at least initially.

Even Jesus Asked First

Do you remember the story of blind Bartimaeus in Mark 10? As Jesus passed him on the road from Jericho, Bartimaeus cried out, "Jesus, Son of David, have mercy on me!" Then Jesus stopped, called for Bartimaeus, and asked him, "What do you want Me to do for you?" (Mark 10:51).

If Jesus, the Lord of all, took time to ask a person in need what they needed, don't you think His actions give us a good model for us to follow? Rather than go into a community, eager to fix all their "problems," the wiser and more dignity-affirming approach is to get to know the people and their customs. Understand why they do what they do. They may teach us a thing or two.

What We Learned

- People have a reason for the things they do.
- When we don't understand a local practice or custom, we should ask if it is beneficial, neutral, or harmful before we take action.
- If we see obvious harmful practices, we should intervene.
- Even Jesus asked people what they wanted from Him.

MYTH: "IF WE DON'T HELP THEM, NO ONE WILL!"

(TRUTH: WE ARE NOT THE SAVIOR.)

I—I am the Lord. Besides Me, there is no Savior.
I alone declared, saved, and proclaimed.

—Isaiah 43:11–12

At a recent training in a local church, a group of development workers was discussing tools we commonly use to assess the needs of people. Just as Jesus at times asked a person in need what they wanted Him to do for them, we as workers need to utilize conversation starter tools that help us ask the same sort of question. For those in the training group whose gifting was more action oriented and who wanted to jump in and start doing something (e.g., digging a well), I could tell the topic was a bit uncomfortable to them.

> Me (to a particular trainee in the group): I can see that you are a bit skeptical about these community development tools.

> Trainee: Yes, I am.

Me: Can I ask why?

Trainee: It seems to me that this approach of interacting with people first takes a long time. Getting to their real problems is a drawn-out process. It's almost a waste of time.

Me: So who is it too slow for? For you or your target community?

Trainee: Truthfully for both, but I guess mainly for the people and community who have all these problems.

Me: These "problems." How long do you think this community has had these problems?

Trainee: Probably for as long as they have been a community.

Me: I agree. Do you think they are aware of their problems? If they are aware, why have they not addressed them?

Trainee: I'm pretty sure they know about some of their problems. I guess they aren't doing anything about them because they can't.

Me: So what do you think will help this community solve their current problems? And how can we equip them to solve the future problems they will face?

Trainee: I'm not sure, but I feel like we need to help them right now. If we don't help them, who will? I'm afraid no one will!

Me: What if we helped this community discover how to solve its own problems? If it is *their* community, *their* problems, and *their* future, shouldn't we help them come up with *their* own solutions?

Trainee: Okay, I'm listening.

Whose Reality Counts?

One of my favorite authors on participatory methods for community development is Robert Chambers. His books constantly challenge the reader to see a community, its problems, and its potential through the eyes of its people. He asserts that this is an essential step to begin to understand what people do and why they do it. And more importantly, viewing reality from the community's perspective should be a part of an overall strategy of participating with the community in whatever solutions emerge.

In one of his best-known books, *Whose Reality Counts: Putting the First Last*, Chambers argues that development workers need approaches that facilitate interaction, learning, and participation with communities instead of top-down instruction and use of science and technology.

Chambers asks of the reader, when working with a community with an eye toward development and improvements,

> Whose knowledge counts?
> Whose values?
> Whose criteria and preferences?
> Whose appraisal, analysis, and planning?
> Whose action?
> Whose monitoring and evaluation?
> Whose learning?
> Whose empowerment?
> Whose reality counts?
> Ours or theirs?[1]

The answer to the last question is "Both." In addressing poverty and basic human needs, we should give priority to the local people's knowledge, values, actions, and even their reality. But we should also recognize that we as outsiders can bring to the situation some insight, experiences, and resources as well. The key is to keep the focus and initiative driving the development process in the hands of the local community.

---

[1] Robert Chambers, *Whose Reality Counts: Putting the First Last* (London: ITDG Publishing, 1997).

We Are Not Called to Be Their Savior

I frequently tell our implementation partners in the field, "The people we are going to work with don't need us to be their savior. They already have one: His name is Jesus." In other words, the communities and people we serve need us to participate with them in the process, not save them from their problems. So we don't go as saviors but partners in the development process.

This is biblical for two reasons. First, there is only one Savior (with a capital S) of the world: Jesus. Second, all people are created in the image of God and share equal value and worth, equal even among the people and populations we work with. In the eyes of God, we are not superior (or inferior) to those we are going to serve in mercy-oriented missions. They may be people with fewer resources than we have in the US. They may have less formal education and less access to basic services. But just like you and me, they are people created in the image of God with amazing potential and creativity. And just like you in me, they are sinners in need of a Savior.

One of the greatest gifts we can offer as we approach cross-cultural ministry missions is the recognition of our own brokenness and need for a Savior. Unwittingly, we tend to ride into underdeveloped communities on what Chambers calls the "three white horses" of development: technology, knowledge, and capitalism. With these in our back pockets, we pop into a community, use those resources to implement our ideas and our projects from the outside, and pop out again as we go home with great stories of how we saved the day.

When we do this, we inadvertently communicate that we (the bringer of answers) and modernity (new technology) will make people's lives better. Don't get me wrong. I like technology. Modern tools often improve life. But true fulfillment in life doesn't come from our gadgets, comforts, or resources.

Koinonia as Participation

In the New Testament, the Greek root word for "community" is *koin*. Its root form implies "having in common." It is where the word *koinonia* comes from. While *koinonia* is generally interpreted as "fellowship," the word can also mean "participation."

This is what Jesus did for us through His incarnation. God became man. He participated in the human experience. He walked among us to show us His love. He lived a life that we could not (a perfect one) and died a death that we deserved so we might know the mercies of God the Father. Jesus became poor for our sake; by His poverty, we may become rich in the knowledge of and relationship with God the Father (2 Corinthians 8:9-10). And His divine power has granted believers the honor of being "partakers" or "participants" with Him in His divine glory (2 Peter 1:3-4). Jesus participated in the human experience so we could experience Him and share in His divine nature.

The greatest gift we can give a developing community is to let them see that we are wholly and wonderfully dependent on God. We are not dependent on technology, knowledge, or capitalism. We have possessions, but those things do not replace the deepest need we have and the deepest need *everyone* has: to be reconciled to God.

The greatest testimony to good community development is that group's sense of ownership over the work. Rather than looking back at what we outsiders swooped in and accomplished, the community should say, "This is what can happen when we utilize the resources around us." We want a community to shoulder the responsibility for their own progress. The same should be said of good evangelism, discipleship, and church multiplication.

An Invitation to Participation

When we as believers feel called to engage in ministry-related missions strategies around the world, we should view it as an invitation to participate with a target community in its development process. We should enter a group as broken and humble people who are totally dependent on God, not on the skills or knowledge we bring to the table. God is inviting us to model and point to dependency on Him for every good gift in our lives. It should be an invitation to leave behind the self-sufficient person and display Spirit-filled lives, wholly reliant on God and looking solely to Him for His plans and His answers.

As Christ participates in our lives, we are called to participate in the lives of others. Our ministry is to help them with all kinds of needs—needs *they* identify and prioritize. Needs that move *them* toward sustainable solutions, mainly utilizing their existing resources. Our mission in this sacred ministry is to simply bear witness to the light as we work alongside them and proclaim, "Be reconciled to God," through Jesus Christ (2 Corinthians 5:20).

A Word of Wisdom from a National Believer

I once participated in a large planning meeting comprised of local (national) believers as well as several Westerners (outsiders). We were grappling with a large-scale problem in that part of the world, an acute issue that was developing into a chronic one due to ongoing armed conflict.

A lot of discussion went back and forth about what kind of resources we Westerners could bring to the situation (or not). There was talk of financial and personnel resources. There was also quite a bit of discussion about how busy we were and the sacrifices required to respond to this amazing but massive opportunity. We all agreed it was a *kairos* moment, a door opened by God to minister to and make known the gospel to a people to whom we had had little access before now. Due to the current conflict, millions of unreached people were fairly easy to interact with as they were being displaced from their homes and even from their country.

As the group (mainly the Westerners) debated the pros and

the cons of what (if anything) could be done, I noticed out of the corner of my eye one of the local believers in the room who had been responding to this need for over a year. He was growing increasingly more agitated by the minute. He had not said anything but simply listened to the ongoing discussions in the room. Finally, he reached a point that he had to speak out.

"I just want to say something. The people in need are not waiting on you to come and help them. They are contacting multiple organizations to help them. You are just a part of their solution. So be relieved of the burden that they depend on you. They are not waking up every morning and mentioning your name. They are poor, but they are not stupid. So do what you can, and depend on God for the rest."

What We Learned

- Believers and churches should be on guard against a savior mentality when we work with people in ministry-related missions. Such an attitude is harmful for the work and for us.
- We have a perception of what is happening in a community, but so does that community—and their perspective is more accurate than ours. We need to yield to *their* views, ideas, and solutions.
- We are not the answer to the world's problems. Jesus is.

MYTH: "IT'S HARD TO TELL A CHURCH MEMBER THEIR IDEA IS BAD."

(TRUTH: IT'S OKAY TO SAY NO.)

Above all, my bothers and sisters, do not swear, either by heaven or by earth or with any other oath. But let your "yes" must mean "yes," and your "no" mean "no," so that you won't fall under judgment.

—James 5:12

My colleague and I visited with a local missions pastor to talk about ways his church and our organization could potentially partner in ministry missions. After introductions, we shared several ideas about how we could work together, from equipping their short-term teams to providing places overseas for teams to work. As we wound down the conversation, we asked the question that we always like to ask to church partners.

Us: Tell us, if we could do one thing to help you, what would it be?

Him: That's a broad question.

Us: Think of it this way. What is the number one problem you face as a minister of missions?

Him (pausing): Well, I do struggle constantly in one area.

Us: Go on.

Him: How do I say no to a church member?

Us: Can you elaborate?

Him: Church members constantly come to me with ideas for ministry projects overseas. Maybe they have met a national believer in their travels or online. Or maybe they sensed a word from the Lord about a certain ministry they want to start. They come to me expecting the church to fully support their idea, from prayer to financing their vision. But honestly, some of the projects and ideas are not that good, and a few of them are potentially harmful. As their missions pastor, I want to affirm them. They care about missions and are actively involved in our church. Many of these folks are committed givers. But I also want to be a good steward of our resources. How do I say no?

Us: That's a good question and frankly one we hear more often than you think.

The Shift in Short-Term Missions

There is an old sports adage that says something like this: "You will miss 100 percent of the shots you don't take." However, in mercy-oriented missions, do we want to do one hundred projects to hit a few good ones? Or is there a better, more effective, and efficient way to approach these projects?

The local church gets bombarded with all kinds of ministry-oriented missions opportunities. A few decades ago, it would have been unusual for a church member to come to the missions leader or team (if you even had one back then) and propose an overseas ministry project. When I was just starting my overseas career in the 1980s, the US church would have seen around 100,000 people globally involved in short-term trips overseas. Today, roughly 1.6 million church members will participate in an overseas missions' experience each year to the tune of almost $2.2 billion.[2] Some have even estimated that US church expenditures on short-term mission trips to be as high as $4 billion annually.[3]

Whatever the numbers, more and more people are exposed to a world in need, which results in more and more resources being poured into overseas projects. Now more than ever, the average church member can see others' needs firsthand and can get involved in cross-cultural missions. The bulk of these efforts leans heavily toward ministry projects like education, orphan care, water systems, etc. It is not uncommon for two or three (or even more) members of a church to be actively engaged in an overseas ministry project. These people may actively promote, raise funds, and mobilize other church members to get involved in their projects.

Short-term missions are a great way to get church members excited, involved, and experienced in fulfilling the Great Commission. However, the church should acknowledge honestly and openly that doing short-term missions is not without its challenges and shortcomings.

Short-term missions give church members hands-on experience in cross-cultural work and ministry. As a result, they often become better givers, prayers, and servants in their local churches when they return. Missions can be a spiritual watershed time for people. It can be a great way to educate church members about the greater world outside the walls of the church and community, and it can give them a more global vision for ministry.

---

[2] Robert Wuthnow and Stephen Offutt, "Transnational Religious Connections," Sociology of Religion 69, no. 2 (2008): 218.

[3] Kurt Ver Beek, "The Impact of Short-Term Missions: A Case Study of House Construction in Honduras after Hurricane Mitch," Missiology: An International Review, Vol. XXXIV, no. 4 (October 2006): 477–495.

Missions experiences also serve as the training ground for our long-term missionary force. Many people who go overseas long term talk about a short-term mission trip that opened their eyes to the needs of the world and played a key role in God's calling on their lives.

Even with all the benefits of a mission trip, the church must ask. "How does our project benefit the people and communities we are serving? What is the overall impact on the areas and population segments where we do missions and ministry? Most importantly, what is the negative impact (potential or real) on the people and communities that are the targets of our mission efforts?" Our church-based mission strategies and efforts frequently overlook this question.

The church also needs to evaluate how these short-term missions experiences might produce negative effects in the local congregation, albeit unintentionally. For example, some short-term projects can divert and dilute a church's resources, weakening its ability to carry out better, more strategic missions efforts. If a church agreed to participate in every proposed project, the resources (money and people) would be spread thin.

Secondly, the church has fostered and exported a Western mentality of missions and development. This problem is not unique to short-term missions, but those efforts have exacerbated the issue.

Please hear me. Short-term mission teams and strategies create good outcomes. Jesus commanded every follower of Jesus to make His name known to the whole. The Great Commission was given to the body of Christ.

But how does the church choose the best and not the lesser? How does it say no to the not-so-good projects and yes to the better ones? How does the missions pastor ensure that the church's resources (money, time, and people) are focused on projects that create a long-term, sustainable change?

As we said to the mission pastor, "That's a good question."

Setting Your Criteria: A Good Place to Start

If you are having trouble deciding which mission projects to support, start with self-analysis. You need to determine your church's priorities, goals, and sweet spots.

It is easy to set priorities, and in ministry mission opportunities, if you define who you are as a church and what goals, objectives, and strategies you want to pursue. While I don't pretend to know you and your church, I would like to offer a few starting points.

1. Base your criteria on biblical standards. I know this sounds elementary, but I am surprised at how easily churches overlook this simple principle. The objective of our mission efforts should be based on scriptural mandates. Does what we do (or propose to do) bring glory to God? Does a project lead to making disciples and the formation of local churches? Does it uphold the value of every person as created in the image of God? Will it lead to worship of the one true God, especially where it was once absent?

2. Incorporate good missiology. Missiology is a fancy term that means "the study of missions." It focuses on good practices in evangelism, discipleship, and church formation, based on what the Bible says about those areas of church life. A good missiology emphasizes the communication of the gospel and healthy ministry approaches, presented in culturally appropriate and understandable ways. Questions to ask about your missions projects include the following: Will the ministry lead to self-sustaining activities and growth among the target population? Will the ministry mission effort empower and develop mature local leaders? Do members of the target group learn to depend on each other and on God, not on your church?

3. Establish clear goals and objectives. Unfortunately, many churches decide to work with a population or people group without a clearly defined outcome in mind. In the quest to help people, churches can launch a missions effort without ever stopping to think about the end

goal. Questions to ask about your goals might be the following: What are the goals and objectives of your group's missions efforts? Whether in proclamation or demonstration of the gospel, are things done with the clear objective of making Christ known? Do your efforts lead to helping more people and giving more people the opportunity to hear the gospel? Answering these questions upfront gives the church clarity in saying yes or no to a particular opportunity or idea.

4. Work from your gifting and sweet spots. Every church has its own DNA of sorts. It has its own unique blending of people with their diverse skills and gifts. Even the church's location (urban or rural, for example) can influence how the church grows and functions. To clarify your church's unique gifting, ask the following: What is your church good at doing? What skills and gifts among the congregation could be utilized for ministry mission projects? For instance, your church may be home to a number of health care professionals who could be cultivated for medical care ministry missions. Perhaps your church is comprised of retired adults who could be trained to serve during a natural disaster. Your church may want to stretch itself and work outside of its known skill sets and gifts, but understand that a project or opportunity that aligns with your sweet spots could garner more support and could be easier to accomplish.

5. Focus on the target group, not your team. The goal of mission endeavors is the proclamation of the gospel, not making church members feel good about helping others. Earlier, I noted some of the positive outcomes of short-term missions. However, there is much debate as to whether these benefits are actual or anecdotal. New evidence suggests that the increasing amount of money being spent on short-term missions does not necessarily result in increasing the numbers of long-term missionaries and strategies.

One good way to measure the viability of a missions project is to evaluate the anticipated benefits as well as the potential damage it could cause the target group. When teams prepare for ministry mission projects, they often pray together and talk about the necessities for the trip. However, few churches evaluate the potential negative impact on the target population.

6. Be affirming but be firm. We as leaders need to be sensitive to fellow church members who are convinced they are pursuing God's will for their lives. However, we also need to be firm and clear about whether their vision of mercy-oriented missions aligns with the church's overall missions philosophy and objectives. We can affirm their calling without getting involved in it.

7. In all things, pray for wisdom and understanding. At the end of the day, we are all human beings and subject to foibles and failures. Even ministers make mistakes—all the time! Praise God, we are not only saved by grace, but we can also live by grace. Pray for God's guidance, listen for His still small voice, and walk as best as you can in His paths.

Three Categories of Supporting Mission Ministry Projects in Our Church

In talking with mission teams and leaders of churches, I have seen three ways they can respond to opportunities for ministry mission projects and opportunities church members present to them.

1. Leaders can bless them and wish them well. If the ministry missions proposal clearly falls outside of a church's goals and objectives, isn't based on good missiology, or simply doesn't fit the church's DNA or giftings, leaders can still give their blessings to the church member who offered the idea. We don't have to literally say no, but we can state clearly that the church will not commit resources (time, people, money) to their project. We can affirm them as individuals but also explain how their project doesn't fit with a church's identity and program. Leaders can bless them to pursue the project God is leading them to do but not partner with them in that project.

2. Churches can participate in a partial but strategic way. If a proposed ministry missions project fits partially with a church's criteria, that church can invest partially. This could involve some financial resources. It might be prayer support and/or offering connections to relationships to help facilitate their vision. It might also involve offering training or even physical goods (like Bibles, literature, etc.) to help with their missions effort.

3. A church can fully partner and adopt the project as a core piece of its missions' strategy. If the proposed ministry mission project aligns well with a church's objectives and goals, then the church can support and endorse it. These projects and strategies would fully align with the church's missions ethos and long-term goals. The church would "own" these missions efforts, promoted and supported fully by the local congregation.

A Word to the Church Member

If God has given you a vision for a particular ministry in mission, it's *your* vision. God is calling *you* to be faithful (or not) to fulfill the vision He gave you. Others might not receive the same calling. That's okay. However, if you continue to encounter resistance from other believers, church leaders, and church staff, you may need to reevaluate. Such feedback may mean that you haven't heard from God as clearly as you thought.

If you go to your missions leaders at your church and pour out your vision for a ministry missions project only to hear that no one wants to get on board, you face a crisis of belief. Do you pursue the vision, or do you drop the plan? Here are a few words of advice.

1. Seek the counsel of others. We all get mixed signals at times. That's okay. That's one of the reasons the body of Christ is so important. Listen to the godly wisdom you hear from those with whom you share your vision. If no one understands the project you believe God

has laid on your heart, go back to the beginning and seek God more. Ask for clarity.

2. If God still leads you to pursue this vision, accept without malice your church's decision to pursue other mission projects. If your vision is of God, He will provide a way for its completion. You don't have to leave the church and find another one to connect with.

3. Ask others what they see (or do not see) in your vision. You may be missing a critical component, or your vision could be off target. Could others bring an element to the project to make it better? Should there be a better biblical basis for it? Or does it not coincide with their individual goals and objectives for ministry mission projects?

4. Ask yourself some difficult questions. Here are some things you need to evaluate: Am I pursuing this because I believe it will help people and expose them to the gospel? Am I doing this because it makes me feel good about myself? What are the short-term and long-term effects on the people and communities I want to serve? Will the local people see the value of what I believe needs to be done? More importantly, do the local people even have my plans on their radar? Have I discussed my plans with leaders in the target community?

Good ministry mission strategies should build up God's kingdom, not tear it down. They should bring people together in unity and cooperation, not drive them apart. And they should result in changed lives both physically and spiritually, and ultimately, they should bring glory to God.

What We Learned

- We need to know our church's identity, its objectives, and its criteria for doing ministry missions in order for it to be able to say yes to the best missions projects.

- Each year, churches and organizations spend a great deal of resources on short-term mission efforts. Church leaders should steward well the resources entrusted to them and seek effectiveness and efficiency in the church's our missions efforts.
- As a missions leader, you can say no to a missions project a church member proposes.
- If you are a church member whose missions leader decline to get involved in your vision and project, that's okay. If God is leading you, He will provide a way for its completion.

MYTH: "TELL US THE ONE THING THAT WILL WORK EVERYWHERE."

(TRUTH: THERE IS NO "ONE SIZE FITS ALL" STRATEGY OR PROGRAM FOR EVERY SITUATION.)

To the Jews I became like a Jew, to win Jews; to those under the law, like one under the law-though I myself am not under the law-to win those under the law. To those who are without the law, like one without the law-not without God's law, but under the law of Christ-to win those without the law. To the weak I became weak, in order to win the weak. I have become all things to all people, so that I may by every possible means save some.

—1 Corinthians 9:20–22

I received a phone call from a church missions leader who needed some assistance.

Missions Leader: We are looking for some help in our overseas missions work.

Me: Excellent! How can we help you?

Missions Leader: We have been involved in a missions partnership with a group of local believers. We have been going to the same place for several years and helping with the local schools, conducting VBS, and doing evangelism outreach door to door. Several people in our group have noticed that there is a lot of hunger and poverty in the communities where we are working and we would like to add a component to our upcoming trip that would help with these issues.

Me: Wonderful! What are you thinking about in particular?

Missions Leader: We are thinking about tacking on two extra days to our trip this year so we can talk to the community and teach them something that will help them have better food and help solve their poverty problems. Can you tell us what will work? Something that could pretty much work everywhere?

The Apostle Paul: All Things to All People

I love the passage quoted at the beginning of this chapter. The apostle Paul told the church at Corinth that he had become "all things to all people" (1 Corinthians 9:22). On the surface, it sounds as if Paul diluted his faith and the gospel in order to gain an audience to share that same gospel. However, this is far from what Paul was communicating in this passage.

While Paul could claim a number of rights as a Christian of Jewish heritage, he willingly gave them up for the sake of the gospel. He could have played the apostle card since he was one of the few remaining people who actually saw the Lord Jesus. The very church to whom he was writing was a living testimony to his effectiveness as an evangelist and church planter.

Yet he made it clear that none of those "rights" were useful to him especially if they put an obstacle in the way of his proclamation of the gospel. He boldly stated in 1 Corinthians 9:19, "Although I am free from all and not anyone's slave, I have made myself a slave to everyone, in order to win more people."

Paul got it. Spreading the gospel was not about him, his accomplishments, or even his programs and agendas. He had become a servant to all, coming alongside them wherever God took him and within whatever relationship he found himself. He identified with that person as closely as possible for the sake of the gospel. Paul made it clear that he did not compromise the gospel. He became as one under the law, but he was not under the law; he was under the grace of Jesus. Yet he became thus in order to win over those under the law.

He became as one outside the law (not outside the law of God but under the law of Christ) that he might win those as well. To the Jew, he became a Jew. To the weak, he became weak. In short, he learned the secret of identifying with those he was trying to reach so that he could gain an audience with those who needed to hear. He simply stated, "Now I do all this because of the gospel, so that I may share in the blessings" (1 Corinthians 9:23).

When we seek to employ ministry missions strategies to engage people for God's kingdom, we would do well to follow Paul's example here. We should seek first to identify with and connect with people, including who they are and where they are. We should leave our prepackaged solutions at home and instead identify with the people we want to reach. We shouldn't quickly offer our opinions about how to "fix" their problems as if we were the heroes.

Clearly, we have the ultimate solution for their most critical need. Every man, woman, girl, and boy in this world needs to know God through the resurrected Christ. Our ministry projects, such as water wells, medical clinics, and poverty alleviation programs, are entry points into the lives and hearts of individuals and communities. These projects are also practical expressions of God's love and mercy and can be a foretaste of God's abundant life both for here and for eternity.

If done correctly—working with people while pointing to God as the source of all good things—our mercy ministry mission projects can be wonderful tools to introduce people to the goodness of God and ultimately the good news of His gospel. If done poorly, our efforts can create distorted messages of God, the nature of humankind, our purpose as human beings, and our potential, rightful, blessed relationship to our Creator.

There Is No Silver Bullet

A "silver bullet" is a metaphor for a simple and easy solution to a complicated problem. Whether a project comes from a Christian group or a secular organization, there is no silver bullet that will bring all people out of poverty, hunger, or whatever problem assailing their community. There is no "one size fits all" solution that, when added with water and stirred, will solve the world's problems. And there is no silver bullet that, when it appears, will make everything better.

We live in a fallen world. That is the story of every life and every community. God created our world for His pleasure and His glory, but our original forefather and foremother (Adam and Eve) made the choice to rebel against God. As a consequence, sin, suffering, and death entered the picture. Our world and everything in it will die; in fact, it is already passing away. But the good news is God promised to create a new heaven and a new earth through His power, and it will be the eternal dwelling place of God with His people.

> God's dwelling is with humanity, and He will live with them. They will be His peoples, and God himself will be with them and will be their God. He will wipe away every tear from their eyes. Death will be no more; grief, crying, and pain will be no more, because the previous things have passed away. (Revelation 21:3–4)

We can seek the "one thing" that will solve the world's suffering, but it won't be a technology or development program we come up with. The one thing and the only thing that ultimately solves the world's problem is the gospel. If we are going to take an answer to the world's problems, it better be couched in this ultimate solution.

Yes, we should strive to help people who are in need and suffering. We should do so in a way that models the truth and reality of who God is and His eternal plan for people and nations. Ministry projects can give us amazing access to people in need, both physically and spiritually. But they cannot, on their own, answer the deepest need of a person or group of persons.

What Can Ministry-Oriented Mission Projects Do for Us? The ABCs

How mercy-oriented ministries can facilitate missions efforts has been articulated as the ABCs in Charles Fielding's book *Preach and Heal: A Biblical Model for Missions.* I shared this information in my book, *Community Development for Kingdom Impact,* but it bears repeating here.

A – Access to unreached (and needy groups). This type of access allows us to go deep in relationship with local people and communities. It gives an opportunity to gain a presence with an audience in need, physically and spiritually. It is biblically based and illustrated best in the life and journeys of the apostle Paul and colleagues.

B – Behind closed doors. This is a safe place away from prying eyes and ears for the gospel to flow. It is an inviting space in their *oikos* or their "household." It leads to the point where Dr. Fielding has described the hosts as "leaning forward," ready to hear the story of life we have to share. "Behind closed doors" can refer to a home, a tent, or even a public area. It is a place where believers can meet and share with the seeker, and where the unbeliever can hear the gospel without the fear of others seeing and passing judgment. Dr. Fielding describes this encounter as "intimate conversation."

C – Care for the needy (and church planting). As we care for the needy with projects, such as benevolent ministries, health care strategies, and hunger initiatives, we demonstrate the gospel in action. However, we do not neglect the proclamation of the gospel. We care for (demonstrate) and share (proclaim) in a seamless manner as to allow the whole message of the gospel to affect the lives of people we help.

D – Disciple-making. The basic command of the Great Commission is to make disciples. It is not simply a command to go. Anyone can travel, but the kingdom development worker goes, ministers, and makes disciples. As Dr. Fielding says, "Authentic disciples are the building blocks of church-planting movements."[4]

In the New Testament, the term *disciple* was the most common name by far given to followers of Jesus Christ. Our goal as modern-day disciples is to minister physically and spiritually and to see the transformation of lives by the power of God's Spirit. Then we can see the newly emerging disciples take the abundant life shared with them and share it with others.

E – Empowering of the (local) church. As it begins to emerge, the local church in a target area is empowered for ministry. The tasks of evangelism, discipleship, and ministry must be instilled in the local community of believers. As people come to faith and begin to form into groups, they need to know they are now a part of the body of Christ and have the same responsibility and calling to reach the unreached as believers in developed areas.

What Is the One Thing That Will Help?

That's easy! Let me quote to you my adapted version of an old Chinese adage credited to Lao Tzu. My additions are in italics.

Go to the people. Live with them. Learn from them. Love them. Start with what they know. Build with what they have.

---

[4] Charles Fielding, *Preach and Heal: A Biblical Model for Missions* (Richmond: International Mission Board, 2008).

Go deep into their culture. Live incarnately with them as Christ lived with us. Show them not only your humanity, but also your utter dependence on God.

But with the best leaders, when the work is done, the task accomplished, the people will say "We have done this ourselves."

And with the best ministry-oriented missions projects, if done in the name of and for the sake of God, the people will say, "To God be the glory."

What We Learned

- There is no "one size fits all" solution to people's problems.
- We should seek to identify with those we want to reach.
- Ministry projects can give us access to people and places, demonstrate the love of Christ and our compassion for people, and create opportunities for evangelism, discipleship, and church planting.

MYTH: "BUT THEY DON'T APPRECIATE WHAT WE'VE DONE FOR THEM!"

(TRUTH: IF YOU ARE DOING MERCY-ORIENTED MISSIONS
FOR APPRECIATION, CHECK YOUR MOTIVES.)

If the world hates you, understand that it hated Me before
it hated you. If you were of the world, the world would love
you as its own. However, because you are not of the world,
but I have chosen you out of it, the world hates you.

—John 15:18–19

I was sitting with a church's missions team that was struggling with several issues. They had been working with an impoverished group for a few years. They had worked in evangelism, discipleship, church planting, and leadership training. They had also done several mercy-oriented mission projects with the local community, including medical clinics, building a water well, and some microenterprise projects.

Me: So tell me how things are going.

Team Leader: It seems to be going well. In fact, we are thinking about moving on from the area and working somewhere else.

Me: Are you thinking about somewhere else in the general area, or maybe a whole new area in a different country?

Team Leader: Actually, we would like to be in the same country and ideally tied to the place where we've been working. We want to get the new believers where we've been working to help in the opening of our new work.

Me: Great idea! Have you started to move this way?

Another Team Member: We've run into a problem. When we brought this up with the community we've been in, they got angry. They said we were abandoning them and that they had a lot of other needs we hadn't met.

Me: How do you feel about this?

A Third Team Member: We feel hurt. We've spent several years working with these people and have done a lot for them. They don't seem to appreciate all that we've done for them.

Missions and Appreciation

We all like to be appreciated. We enjoy the approval of a supervisor, family member, or coworker. We'll even accept praise from a complete stranger! However, here's a difficult truth to accept: We are not called to be on mission with God for the sake of appreciation. We are called to be on mission to bear witness to God's glory so people from all tongues, tribes, and nations will worship the only One worthy of praise and adoration: Almighty God.

Everything that believers do and everything we are should be about making Christ known.

- Our efforts to provide clean water for people should be a picture of and a platform to share the truth of the One who can quench our eternal thirst.
- Our providing food in a disaster should meet critical needs, but it should also help make known the One who is the Bread of Life.
- Our strategies in health care should not only help people live better and healthier lives but also lead to conversations about the One who can heal the sin-sick soul.

In short, our ministry-oriented mission efforts do not focus on us or our desires. Missions centers on the needs of lost people, both their physical and (especially) their eternal needs. It concentrates on showing the love and purpose of God tangibly to those in need, as well as holding forth the truth of who He is and His plan for salvation. We meet people's present needs and point to the One who can meet their eternal needs.

Jesus said He came so we might "have life and have it in abundance" (John 10:10). This is a unifying theme for followers of Jesus—to help people who are suffering under the curse of a fallen world. In the name of Jesus, we can help mothers feed their children. We can help widows and orphans live with dignity and relative security. We can provide better health care for those who have little or no access to it. All while proclaiming the message "Be reconciled to God" (2 Corinthians 5:20).

So if you and I are doing missions for appreciation, I have a simple solution: stop it.

Jesus's Job Description for His Disciples

Today's American culture values safety and comfort. We enjoy our modern conveniences, and our decision-making processes center around risk aversion and security.

However, if we created a biblical job description for the follower of Jesus, we would find some elements that go against our culture and, in many cases, our human nature. A brief version of what we can expect when we faithfully follow Jesus can be found in Matthew 10:16–23.

- "Look, I'm sending you out like sheep among wolves" (v. 16).
- "Beware of them, because they will hand you over to local courts and flog you in their synagogues."
- "You will even be brought before governors and kings because of Me" (v. 18).
- "Brother will betray brother to death, and a father his child. Children will even rise up against their parents and have them put to death" (v. 21).
- "You will be hated by everyone because of My name" (v. 22).

In Luke's gospel, Jesus said,

Then He said to them all, "If anyone wants to follow after Me, let him deny himself, take up his cross daily, and follow Me. For whoever wants to save his life will lose it, but whoever loses his life because of Me will save it." (Luke 9:23–24)

The Bible is clear: comfort, security, and appreciation are not promised to those who follow Jesus. In fact, the opposite often occurs.

But People Will Take Advantage of Us!

People will take advantage of believers. This is true. That's what unregenerate people do. However, Jesus taught us how to relate to those who would take advantage of us.

On the contrary, if anyone slaps you on your right cheek, turn the other to him also. As for the one who wants to sue you and take away your shirt, let him have your coat as well. And if anyone forces you to go one mile, go with him two. Give to the one who asks you, and don't turn away from the one who wants to borrow from you. (Matthew 5:39–42)

You have heard that it was said, "Love your neighbor and hate your enemy." But I tell you, love your enemies and pray for those who persecute you, so that you may be children of your Father in heaven … Be perfect, therefore, as your heavenly Father is perfect. (Matthew 5:43–44, 48)

Everyone Has an Agenda (Whether We Know It or Not)

Christians are often offended and even shocked when we run into people and communities with ulterior motives. Unfortunately, this is a common problem in cross-cultural settings with our teams. They are some of the hardest working people in the world, highly called and sacrificing to work and minister in a strange, foreign culture. Even in that setting, believers must reckon with the reality that people don't always have the best of motives in mind when interacting with others. It is a good reminder for your church's missions efforts as well.

This is not a cynical way of looking at the world. People just like you and I have ideas, dreams, and goals in life, and sometimes their motives are altruistic and pure. Sometimes their motives are less than pure. As believers go across the street and around the world and implementing ministry-based missions, we will meet people whose agenda may be different from ours.

Part of the reason for such an agenda stems from working in poor communities that have been shaped by what I call a "poverty" worldview or a scarcity mindset. In this perspective, the world contains a limited amount of "goodness" or resources. They think of it like a pie. The whole pie represents all of the goodness in the world.

If you get a bigger slice, then I am probably going to get a small one. It is not fair that you get a bigger slice, or more resources, than I do.

In some overseas settings where I have worked, the concept of "borrowing" was a way to even out the disproportionate pie slices. I worked with people who had a lesser pie slice, or fewer resources, than I did as a Westerner. If someone wanted to borrow one of my tools, I should be happy to lend it and not be too upset if it didn't come back. The person who borrowed the tool might lend it to a friend who needed it. I wasn't using it anyway, and I had lots of tools lying around, so it was no big deal. I could even go and buy another one if I wanted, so permanently "borrowing" from me was acceptable.

When churches enter a community or new area to work, that community has already formed preconceived ideas about who we are and what we can or can't do. Those ideas may be correct, or they may be completely false. The notions could be based on the dozens of other foreigners and groups who have been to that community before. I know it is hard to accept, but we are rarely the first ones to a place. It's okay. There's no shame in being second (or forty-fifth).

These new (to us) communities have survived a long time, even centuries in some cases. They have seen outsiders like us come and go. They are generally hospitable (a highly held value in many cultures) and patient. After all, these communities want to see what this new group will offer to their community. In fact, some places and people in the world have perfected the art of entertaining foreigners and mission groups as a viable way to bring in resources to their communities.

Seems cynical, doesn't it? It sounds as if bad people with hidden agendas are waiting to pounce on a church's good intentions and missionary efforts. The truth is the Western church has helped to create much of this dysfunctional relationship with communities in need. Unfortunately, many of our churches and people's well-meaning efforts have had a shortsighted vision of ministry-oriented missions and actually perpetuated the problem.

What about Our Agenda?

Everyone has an agenda—even a believer or a church. We have an agenda in our ministry-oriented missions projects. Our motives may be pure, but sometimes they are not. Our agendas include

- helping people in need
- sharing the gospel
- being obedient to Christ and His Word
- going on an overseas adventure
- guilt over materialism while other people live in poverty
- travel
- building a resumé
- experiencing other cultures
- romantic interest in someone else on the team
- _____ (You can name a dozen more.)

People can have agendas. It's okay. What's not okay is to close our eyes to this fact.

Awareness of this can help us better understand the people we work with. It can also help us better understand ourselves as we go.

What We Learned

- We should not do ministry missions for what we get out of it. We should do it to help people in need and make Christ known.
- Almost everyone has an agenda, and that's not necessarily a bad thing. Ignoring that fact is far more dangerous than acknowledging it.
- Even believers have an agenda as we do ministry-oriented missions. We desire to make Christ known by our actions (caring for people's needs) and our words.

MYTH: "WE HELPED ONE FAMILY AND NOW THE REST OF THE COMMUNITY HATES US."

(TRUTH: SEEK TO UNDERSTAND THE LOCAL CULTURE AND HOW YOUR ACTIONS AFFECT IT.)

**There is a way that seems right to a person,
but its end is the way to death.**

—Proverbs 14:12

Our efforts to implement mercy-oriented ministry projects in a cross-cultural setting don't always lead to the results we want. A huge reason for this is that we outsiders don't take time to understand local cultures and community decision-making processes before implementing "our" plans. A recent discussion with a church member who had a lot of experience doing mission projects illustrates this problem.

Her: We've run into a problem with one of our projects.

Me: Can you tell me about it?

Her: We have been working in a community for a long time and have great relationships. Everyone seems to like us, and we have done a lot of good.

Me: Okay.

Her: But last year, we helped an elderly man by building him a new home and then everything changed.

Me: Go on, please.

Her: Well, it started out good. The old man was a widower and didn't have much family. The place he was living was a dump, not fit for a human to live in. We met him because he had attended some of our medical clinics in the past. Some of our team members got to know him better, and our hearts were broken over his living situation. When we returned home after one trip, we decided to build him a new home. It didn't cost much, and our church was happy to provide the funds. During the next trip, we shared our plan with the man and the church we were working with, and everyone seemed happy with the idea.

Me: So what's the problem?

Her: As we completed the house, several of the church members approached us and wanted houses built for them as well. We explained to them that this was a one-off project and we built the old man a house because he really needed one. The church members then told us that they needed new houses and it wasn't fair for us to help only one person. They even said that he wasn't a good church member and we should help the them (the good members) if we were going to help anyone. People in the church have started treating the old man badly, and the community seems to be punishing him for getting a new house.

Me: What do you think you are going to do? How will you address the feelings of the other people in the community?

Her: We can't build a house for everyone! We're not sure what to do next.

Seek to Understand First before Being Understood

An axiom that I oftentimes remind churches when working with people in need, especially cross-culturally, is "Seek to understand before being understood."

Too often, we outsiders come in, judge a situation, and create solutions based on what we see on the surface. Moved with compassion and a cultural propensity for moving quickly and getting things done, we lean toward making quick decisions and taking action. Decisiveness and aggressive action win the day always, don't they?

Not always.

Sometimes swift action is good, especially in America, an individualistic-oriented culture. But in community-based cultures with a collective outlook on life and decision-making processes, "fast" and "to the point" can be counterproductive, even harmful. And in the eyes of that culture, such quick responses are considered downright rude.

I am happy for the old man who received a home. But what if that church had taken some time and explored the deeper reasons for his poor living situation? The situation might have turned out better if the church had involved the community in the thought process from the beginning. They probably could have avoided some of the misunderstanding and resentment from the rest of the community.

Getting the Community Involved Usually Pays Dividends

Through the years, I have learned that getting a population involved in evaluating problems and solutions in its own community usually provides a more complete picture of the issues at hand. If done well, it can also help outsiders sidestep landmines in the process.

We as Westerners don't like to slow down and get consensus when there are so many pressing problems. However, remember that the target community has been there a long time before you and I arrived, and it will exist long after we leave. Its people have lived for generations without outside help. Long-term and systemic change takes time, so your church can pause to understand the situation before launching into your amazing program.

A recent disaster response reinforced this approach. A massive earthquake caused extensive damage in an Asian country. It left many dead and even more injured, but the largest effect was the destruction of infrastructure, especially to people's homes. To make matters worse, the earthquake occurred just before the start of the rainy season, so the survivors knew the floods were coming and they had few options for shelter.

Along with several other organizations, our group launched a temporary housing program to provide basic shelter from the elements. We knew more permanent housing would be necessary, but we took our time before moving forward. First, and to be totally transparent, we wanted to get a solid estimate on how many dollars would come in through our donors. After meeting emergency needs of food, water, shelter, hygiene kits, and medicines, we wanted an estimate of how much we might have left for a home construction project.

Second, and most importantly, previous disasters had taught us the value of involving local people in the process of making decisions on a project. They helped us decide where to work (priority areas), who should and shouldn't receive a home based on need and/or merit, and crucially, what the home would look like. The local leadership helped us determine a standard model that would be culturally appropriate. We also talked about what they would contribute to the process and what kind of housing design the local and national government give would approve.

I have witnessed horror stories in which outside organizations move into an area after a disaster and started building houses largely based on what they think local people need. Many of these groups bring in prefabricated houses made of cheap materials. While they are safe and easy to install, the "horror" part to this story is no one usually lives in these structures. Today, I can take you to countries where "model villages" were constructed without insider input, and they are still vacant or used as animal housing or storage.

Please don't hear me criticizing the projects of others. *Do* hear me say that the best projects and programs involve and empower local people. Local preferences and buy-in are important in disaster recovery, even after the critical stage has ended.

In the large earthquake event I referenced earlier, the communities reached a point when they were ready to establish their new homes. My team discussed several options with them. They wanted to rebuild their previous existing homes, but our resources could not make that possible. We agreed to help them with a simple shelter/ home. The new homes wouldn't be the same size as what they'd lost, but families could expand as their resources allowed. The agreement was a standard shelter per each qualifying family with a counterpart contribution by the family receiving the new structure. Together we decided on a metal frame with exterior siding and a tin roof. Its dimension would be sixteen feet by twenty feet and would have three eight-foot by ten-foot rooms (roughly) and an open porch of the same dimensions.

As a counterpart, each family provided the building site for the new house. The local people also agreed to prepare the foundation, which could be as simple as compacted earth or a cement slab. They also agreed to construct a three-foot concrete (or cement-block) wall around the perimeter of the foundation. The community helped choose where and with whom to start the work. Priority was given to the most destitute families, which made us as the outsiders glad. Also, they set the rules to be followed in order for house construction to proceed. If a family did not provide the site and foundation with the perimeter wall, it did not get a house. In cases of a widow with no family, the community pitched in and did her part.

Being a person of little faith, I didn't think we would get a high level of participation. Out of six hundred homes needing to be constructed, I thought we would be doing good to get a 50 percent participation rate. The requirements the community placed on its members were stiff.

I was proven wrong (shown to have little faith). Only a handful of households did not complete the requirements and dropped out of the project. The project had about a 99 percent success and participation rate. I credit this to a great team but also because we took time to get community involvement from the beginning.

Community-Oriented Cultures versus Individual-Oriented Cultures

We (Westerners) live an individual-oriented culture. We make decisions based on personal judgments and desires. We value the person who is "self-made." We love to see individuals rise above their circumstances and become heroes and role models for the rest of us.

By contrast, most developing countries and impoverished sectors of the world are community oriented or collective cultures. They make decisions more based on the welfare of the community over the individual. They would see success not as individuals overcoming their circumstances, but rather communities rising up together as a whole.

Here are some basic characteristics and differences between an individual-oriented culture and a collective culture. This list is by no means comprehensive and adapted from David Livermore's excellent book on doing short-term missions, *Serving with Eyes Wide Open: Doing Short-Term Missions with Cultural Intelligence*.[56]

---

[5] [6] David Livermore, *Serving with Eyes Wide Open: Doing Short-Term Missions with Cultural Intelligence* (Grand Rapids: Baker Books, 2006).

Individual-Oriented Society	Collective-Oriented Society
values personal achievement	values group achievement
thrives on competition	thrives on cooperation
regards individual rights as most important	regards good of the group as most important
seeks independence and individual success	seeks interdependence and group success
tends to be more guilt-oriented	tends to be more shame oriented
encourages people to rely on themselves	encourages people to rely on each other
values spontaneous and impulsive decisions; high risk	values calculated and consensus decisions; low risk

This is merely a cursory discussion regarding the differences between individualism and collectivism, and there are many books on the subject. The point is a culture's values and worldview dictate our approach to working with communities in cross-cultural ministry missions.

What We Learned

- Most of us live in an individualistic culture. We need to learn about the thought patterns, decision-making processes, and values of other cultures.
- Churches and missions groups need to slow down and take time to understand the perspective of the target community. This approach will lead to better long-term outcomes.
- We need to understand before trying to be understood.

MYTH: "WE DON'T WANT THEM TO BECOME DEPENDENT ON US."

(TRUTH: DEPENDENCY IS NOT A FOUR-LETTER WORD.)

He is the image of the invisible God, the firstborn over all creation. For everything was created by Him, in heaven and on earth, the visible and the invisible, whether thrones or dominions or rulers or authorities—all things have been created through Him and for Him. He is before all things, and by Him all things hold together.

—Colossians 1:15–17

The word *dependency* has become a four-letter word in many missions circles. Some groups simply don't address needs of people and communities in their target areas, choosing to focus solely on the "higher" calling of evangelism, discipleship, and church planting. They choose to let the physical needs go unmet, fearing they could become distracted from the main purpose of their mission—sharing the gospel. Feeding the hungry, taking care of the poor, providing health care services, and other mercy-oriented efforts would take away from the priority proclamation mandate.

Most who hold this view see the new believers in these target areas as the ones responsible to address the needs in the community as a part of the local church's mandate. They would see their primary role as proclamation, discipleship, and church formation. Anything (e.g., ministry projects) that would distract them from this role would slow down their efforts.

Below is a conversation I had with a church planter friend living and working overseas.

> Me: I see you're working in an area with a lot of poverty and hunger. Have you thought about ways to incorporate ministry projects into your strategies?
>
> Him: Yes, there are a lot of needs in my target group, but I've decided not to get involved with those so I can stay focused on my discipleship groups.
>
> Me: Have you considered how you can make a ministry project a part of your discipleship program? You could teach the believers about sharing their faith, multiplying disciples, forming churches, and ministering to those in need. You'd be teaching them to obey everything Jesus commanded.
>
> Him: I believe the people I am discipling will do those ministry projects later when they become a church. It is the local church's responsibility to meet needs, not mine.
>
> Me: I agree. The local church can and should be about mercy ministries in the community and they should do this in the name of Jesus. But I wonder what we are modeling for them.
>
> Him: What do you mean?
>
> Me: If we share the gospel, lead them to Jesus, teach them how to share their faith, form churches, and rapidly multiply, but we fail to model the basics of Jesus's teaching, like loving

neighbors and caring for the widow, orphan, and stranger, what kind of Christianity are we modeling? People learn from what I teach, but they learn a lot more by how I live and what I do.

Him: Maybe so. But I am afraid of creating dependency on us. We don't want them to rely on us for things like food and medicine. The needs here are so massive we would get quickly overwhelmed if we opened that door. We don't want them to be dependent on us, so we are careful not to do much in the way of mercy ministries.

Me: So dependency is bad?

Him: Absolutely.

Me: But is that fair? The target group and the new believers you are working with have huge physical needs. You are teaching the gospel among them, but only addressing their spiritual needs. What about their hungry children? What about their inability to obtain simple treatment for sicknesses? If you and I introduce people to a God who cares, but we don't care to alleviate their suffering, are we misrepresenting the gospel?

Him: Maybe.

Reasons We Are Afraid of Dependency

In truth, we are all dependent on God. For every breath, for every second of life. If not for the provision and grace of God, we would cease to exist. The problem comes when we as believers portray ourselves as self-made, independent Westerners who don't have to depend on God. We can utilize an amazing support system, education base, and connections to solve our problems. We don't mean to, but we send a mixed message to those we are called to reach.

People come to us with their problems and we generally respond in one of two ways. We either say, "I'm only here to tell you about the gospel," or we say, "Let me help you," emphasizing *our* role in fixing their problems. Of course, we don't use those actual words, but our responses and actions say it for us. While the Bible and the example of Jesus's life exhort us over and over to participate in the lives of those in need—to share the gospel *and* care for the needy—we wrestle with fears and misconceptions about how to live that out. Here are a few reasons why we are afraid to engage with others' tangible needs:

1. Meeting needs will take away time and effort from our main goals: evangelism, discipleship, and church planting. This is probably the most common fear, largely birthed out of our Western, dualistic worldview. However, if we see our task as making Christ known in all we say and do, we can develop a more wholistic approach to gospel proclamation that verbalizes "be reconciled to God" while also caring for people's needs in a way that models and leads to such reconciliation. Jesus sent out His disciples to proclaim, "The kingdom of heaven has come near" (Matthew 4:17), while also healing the sick and caring for those in need. Believers can (and should) do the same, in no way compromising the proclamation of the gospel.

2. The needs are too enormous. When believers look at massive needs like poverty, hunger, and health issues, we can become overwhelmed and paralyzed into inaction. The fear is that if we start down the road of addressing these massive problems, they may overwhelm us and consume all of our time. This would prevent us from doing the main things like evangelism, discipleship, and church planting.

Again, a great model for dealing with the masses' needs is Jesus. He looked at the crowds and was moved with compassion (Matthew 9:36; Matthew 14:14), but He also listened for the cry of the individual. When Jesus met the needs of people, He almost always focused on an individual, not the masses. And in most of those instances, He combined His healing and ministry with the proclamation of the good news. The lesson is this: let the needs of the masses move us to action, but let us also find ways to meet the needs of individuals in the love and name of Christ.

3. We don't want to make "rice Christians." This term comes from the olden days of missions in the Far East. During times of great famine, missionaries in a certain area were accused of providing rice to the hungry as a way to coerce people into conversion. Governments and religious groups around the world make similar claims today. No pressure exists in the majority of these cases. When the love of Christ is expressed in a tangible way and people hear the gospel, it is the *gospel* that draws people and not the food. However, churches and groups still fear that people will appear to accept the message in exchange for a perceived benefit (like rice).

The solution is simple: don't coerce. Help people in need. Work with local leaders and community-based programs. Listen to the target group, participate with them in their struggles, and be transparent about who you are as a believer and why you are helping them. As God gives you opportunities, talk about your faith and challenge people to "be reconciled to God" because "the kingdom of heaven has come near."

4. I don't have the necessary skills. "I'm not a disaster response expert." "I faint at the sight of blood, so I can't participate in health care ministries." "I can't get a handle on what needs to be done." These are all valid arguments and reactions to the needs of others. But that's why churches and groups work in teams. That's also why churches can partner with national believers to model a more wholistic picture of ministry missions. This approach allows churches to listen to local partners, learn from them, come alongside them, and participate with them in ministering and proclaiming in a mercy-oriented way.

5. I'm already overburdened. There are needs for my family. I am busy with other tasks. I am struggling just to survive with this new language and culture. Or we only have ten days for our mission trip! These are real issues that may tempt us to take shortcuts in our work and bypass healthy processes in our mercy ministry efforts, which could lead to bad practices and dependency.

If these are struggles you face, I would encourage you to pray for discernment, ask God to clarify how He is leading you, and ask Him to open your eyes and ears to the opportunities to meet needs and make His name known.

A Healthier View of Dependency

What if, from the very beginning of working with people in mercy-oriented missions, we as believers decided that dependency could be a *good* thing and a potentially positive outcome? We don't want people to depend on Western outsiders, but we do want community members to depend on each other and ultimately God. What if we as believers entered a community with transparency about our dependency on God? Would it make a difference for a community to see believers humbly trusting in the grace and goodness of God rather than our own resources?

1. Such an approach would help eliminate the Savior mentality that we believers sometimes carry with us onto the mission field.
2. Demonstrating dependence on God would also help remove some of the fear and burden we feel because of the massive needs we see but can't eradicate.
3. Living in dependence on God also would help believers be more authentic and truthful with the people we have been called to serve.

Bad versus Good Dependency

In our mercy-oriented missions efforts, some dependencies can be "good," while others can be "bad."

Good Dependency	Bad Dependency
The local people depend on one another to find resources for and solutions to their problems.	The local people depend on outsiders (believers) to find resources for and solutions to their problems.
The local community forms relationships with many organizations. It taps local and national government resources to accomplish its goals. It forms partnerships with other nongovernment organizations and builds relationships with institutions nearby who can help provide local solutions to its problems.	The local community forms an exclusive relationship with a specific church or organization and looks to it every time it encounters a new need.
The local people see that we (the outsiders) are broken and in need of a Savior, just like they do. They see our resources, but they also have seen that we are dependent on the grace and mercy of God because we have modeled this attitude for them.	The local people begin to view outsiders as the answer to all their problems. They see how strong we Westerners are, the amazing resources we bring to the table, and how successful we are, and they want to emulate us.

Paternalism versus Dependency

Steve Corbett and Brian Fikkert have written an excellent book entitled *When Helping Hurts*. Its goal is to speak to the church, especially in the United States, to address the issue of alleviating poverty without hurting the target community (and ourselves) in the process.

Corbett and Fikkert highlight an often hidden (to us outsiders) problem called paternalism. Paternalism is doing for others what they can do for themselves. Such efforts are often well-intentioned, but they can leave people dependent upon others and even rob them of the motivation and joy of handling their own problems. This "help" also "hurts." It leads to stunted or handicapped growth of individuals and communities. The authors identified five forms of paternalism,[67] to which I add a sixth (below).

1. Resource paternalism. This stems from a Western "have" and "have not" philosophy of poverty. If we see the poor of the world as lacking things, we will be tempted to provide the "things" or resources. While our intentions are good, this response actually cripples a community's ability to grow in its development.

2. Spiritual paternalism. When Western believers assume a position of spiritual superiority, we miscommunicate what the kingdom of God is about. We should embrace other followers of Jesus as equals and recognize that the Holy Spirit works through them in their culture in a more relevant way than we outsiders can. Over and over, I have been amazed at the spiritual insights I learn from national partners if I will only listen. The one thing we do is continually point them to the Word of God for direction, and we should be open to how God speaks to them (and their culture) through His scriptures.

3. Knowledge paternalism. We as outsiders often assume a community is underdeveloped because it lacks knowledge. Early on, I learned to view local people as a whole lot smarter than I am. They could live in harsh environments with limited resources. If I tried to duplicate what they were doing, I would not survive. For instance, I learned

---

[67] Steve Corbett and Brian Fikkert, *When Helping Hurts: How to Alleviate Poverty without Hurting the Poor* (Chicago: Moody Publishers, 2014).

that even though I was a college-trained agriculturalist, the Filipino farmers I worked with were far more capable of living and existing in their conditions. They could raise a family of six on two acres of land with only a net cash flow of US $25 per month. They could feed, clothe, house, and educate their children. I came to regard them as some of the smartest people in the world. I concluded, rightfully so, that I could not do what they did with the resources they had.

4. Labor paternalism. Labor paternalism is the tendency to see people as helpless and unable to contribute anything (such as labor) to the solution of their biggest problems. When we outsiders assume local people and communities have nothing to contribute to their development process, we are tempted to take over, not only procuring the resources for the community but also bypassing the one thing they can contribute (in many cases): their labor.

5. Managerial paternalism. This type of paternalism can manifest itself in the planning and implementation steps of the community development process. We trust the community to identify its problems and come up with solutions. However, we outsiders take over the implementation and monitoring of their project(s). These actions come from a deep-seated belief that the poor community cannot be good managers, as evidenced by their current conditions. We outsiders must avoid this type of paternalism if we want the community to take charge and move forward with its development.

6. Cultural paternalism. This is probably the most hidden and thus dangerous form of paternalism. We are all ethnocentric, meaning that we believe (either consciously or subconsciously) that our way of doing things is "right." We succumb to this belief because, at the core, everyone interprets life and circumstances from their own cultural framework. Our ethnocentricity makes it hard to trust others' way of doing things. In terms of community development, it tempts us to step into the process and circumvent the decision-making process and choices of a group of people. We as outsiders need to guard

our hearts, motives, and actions so we don't impose our cultural understanding and choices on the people with whom we are working.

One of the core principles in training community development workers to overcome cultural paternalism is to evaluate every question and decision through the lens of scripture. This approach reminds us that we don't know all the answers, and it demonstrates to a community that we are people of biblical principles and faith. It sets an example for the community to look to God's Word for answers.

The Local Church: A Model of Dependency and Interdependency

In missions, our goal is to bear witness to the glory of God. We want our evangelism efforts to lead to disciple-making. We want those disciples grouped together to form New Testament churches. And we want to see those new believers and churches joyfully reproducing and sharing the truth of the gospel and their abundant life with others.

Everything we do is to see Christ proclaimed. We use our words and God's Word to hold forth the truth. We use acts of mercy and compassion to show people who God is and what His plan is for them. We tell others that God is gathering together a redeemed people and kingdom for Himself so that He will ultimately receive the glory due to Him and Him alone. He is accomplishing this through the faithful sacrifice of His Son, Jesus, and through the ministry of reconciliation He entrusted to the body of Christ, the church.

The New Testament church is the perfect model of dependency and interdependency. The body doesn't exist and function without a head. Jesus is the head—the Author, Sustainer, and Fulfillment—of the church. Everything is from Him, through Him, and for Him (Colossians 1:16). The body is interdependent on its parts. Can the hand say to the foot, "I don't need you?" Or the leg to the arm, "I want nothing to do with you?" (1 Corinthians 12:12–27).

Are you afraid of dependency? It's okay to be scared, but don't let that fear dictate your actions. Remember you and I are totally dependent on God. And as the body of Christ, believers are dependent on each other. Our dependency is a model for those we want to reach.

What We Learned

- Dependency is not necessarily bad.
- Some types of dependency are good, but other kinds of dependency are unhealthy.
- Dependency in the form of paternalism can be harmful to those we are trying to help. We should not do for others what they can do for themselves.
- We are all dependent on the goodness and the grace of God, whether we have abundant or scant resources.
- As the body of Christ, the church depicts a beautiful picture of dependency on God and interdependency on each other.

MYTH: "WHAT WE'VE DONE WILL FALL APART WHEN WE LEAVE!"

(TRUTH: DON'T TAKE OWNERSHIP OF WHAT BELONGS TO OTHERS.)

But as it is, God has arranged each one of the parts in the body just as He wanted. And if they were all the same part, where would the body be? As it is, there are many parts, but one body.

—1 Corinthians 12:18–20

A local church wanted to sit down with me to talk about their mercy-oriented missions work overseas. For the past five years, the church had been making two to three trips a year to a particular place. Things had been going well. The church had done a lot of evangelism and discipleship and seen some good results. It had also done a variety of ministry projects, from building a water well to hosting medical clinics to conducting income-generating projects. However, the church perceived that its time in the community was ending, and the church was finding it difficult to exit.

Missions Pastor: We want to find a way to leave this area to do work elsewhere, but every time we bring up the subject, our church expresses a lot of concerns.

Me: What kind of concerns?

Missions Pastor: For one, we have developed so many great relationships and have made so many friends that it's painful to think about moving on to another work.

Me: Could you do both? Could you move on to do other work and still encourage some of your folks visit this community from time to time?

Missions Pastor: We have talked about that.

Me: Something else seems to be troubling you.

Missions Pastor: Our biggest fear is that when we leave this area, everything we did in the community will fall apart.

Me: How so?

Missions Pastor: We won't be there to keep things going. We are helping them with their pastor training, income-generating projects, and even their church outreach programs.

Me: When you say you're helping, do you mean your church is providing the funding?

Missions Pastor: Yes, we are funding their work, but we are also providing the leadership for the work. It seems as if the church waits until we arrive to make major decisions for its work and ministries. We've tried to encourage local leaders to take responsibility, but it seems like the church always waits for our arrival so we can make the decisions for them. We don't want to do it for them, but they don't seem to want to take leadership roles. We find ourselves constantly pushing the programs and the decisions.

Me: It sounds a lot like driving a vehicle with a flat tire and running alongside it as it moves to pump up the tire constantly.

Missions Pastor: Exactly! If we leave, we're afraid everything we've done will fall apart.

Sustainability Begins with Ownership

Along with participation and transformation, sustainability is one of the keys looked for when trying to determine whether or not our efforts resulted in good community development. Is the work "sustainable"? In other words, will the work result in continued efforts, momentum, and lasting impact in a community once we as outsiders leave?

In evangelism, disciple-making, and church planting circles, missiologists talk about reproducibility and multiplication. The goal is for the people we have worked with to pick up the gospel mandate, just like us, and carry it on themselves.

Sustainability (or reproducibility) begins with ownership. In making disciples and planting churches, people who come to faith and form churches should be trained and equipped to replicate their faith by sharing their testimonies, presenting the gospel, and living out kingdom principles in their families and places of influence. These local believers need to own their faith and share what God has done for them, even from the earliest moments after their initial conversion. Outside church planters can provide training and equipping for the new believers as they practice their newfound faith, but these believers need to take responsibility for their faith and the ministry of reconciliation.

The same is true for mercy-oriented mission projects. When outsiders approach communities with relief and development strategies to address hunger, poverty, poor health, and other issues, we must find ways from the beginning to ensure ownership of the problems and the ensuing solutions remain in the hands of the local people. After all, whose problem is it? Whose solution should it be?

The Fallacy of "Turning Over" a Project

If we as outsiders never take on the community's problems and solutions as our own, we never have to worry about ownership issues. We keep the focus on the community, their perceptions, their desires, and most importantly, what course of action they take (or not) in solving what they see as priority issues.

A common mistake we as outsiders make is when we design solutions to people's problems from a distance. We build a better water filter in our laboratories and then take it to a world in need to sell our system. We sit in our offices and think about how solar power can solve the world's energy crisis, design a portable battery charger, and then try to convince impoverished nomads in the desert to use our solution. Or we come up with a new way to package or preserve food to solve world hunger and promote it as the way to feed all the hungry people in the world.

None of these technologies or their many variations are bad, although some are better than others. Technology is neutral in and of itself, but it doesn't solve the problems that communities face. How we approach people and communities from the very beginning to hear their thoughts, ideas, and dreams is more critical to the success of a project than the technology used.

When I hear the statement (in various forms) "We are going to start a project with our target people, show them how to do it, and then turn it over to them," I know problems lie ahead. In general, outsiders don't have success when we turn over projects to local people and communities. If we turn over something, we made all the key decisions and designs to the project or strategy. We may run it successfully in their presence, and we may have worked with a local person or two who showed aptitude for that project. But in the end, if we turn over a project, it was ours from the beginning.

I propose a much better approach. Outsiders should never take ownership out of the hands of the local people or community. Unless the project is a response to a disaster event and/or a life-threatening situation, outsiders need to keep their hands off the ownership role. Let it be of the community—for the community and by the community.

As outsiders, we can be a catalyst. We can be a facilitator in the community development process. We can participate in their suffering and struggles to find locally sustainable and culturally appropriate solutions to their most pressing needs. But we outsiders need to let them discover their own problems, prioritize them, design their own solutions, and implement their own plans. If the local people own the work from the beginning to the end of the process, we will never need to plan a turnover ceremony, and the likelihood of sustainability increases a thousandfold.

An Example of a Mercy-Oriented Ministry Project in the US

This approach could work in the US church. For example, many churches run a food pantry or clothes closet to help those in the community who are in need. Most of the time, church members with the gift of mercy or service run these ministries, which are typically open one or two days a week. Generally, the individual church sets up these ministries, the guidelines for who qualifies for assistance, and provides the labor and management to run the ministry.

Another approach to these ministries could accomplish the same result but with a greater impact: get the beneficiaries involved in the whole process. What if a church were to find a way to involve potential recipients in the design, setup, guidelines, and oversight of a food or clothes distribution ministry? Such a project wouldn't even need to be housed in the church but could instead be located off-site. This might also be a way to provide paying jobs for those needing help, which would give them dignity as they provide for their own needs and the needs of their families.

This different approach is popping up in some places in the US. It is not a perfect solution, nor is it problem free. In fact, it is a lot messier than a church setting up and controlling the ministry from the beginning. However, inviting recipients to participate in and even own the process takes advantage of their perspective, empowers them to make decisions, and allows them to be a part of the solution. Doing ministry this way does require a paradigm shift for the church. It requires more work and deeper, ongoing relationships with those involved in the process. However, it can create a more lasting impact on the lives of the recipients as well as a deeper avenue to share the gospel.

An Example of a Mercy-Oriented Ministry Project Overseas

On a recent visit to South Asia, I saw a successful project forming self-help groups (SHGs) in impoverished communities. These target areas were extremely poor, even by the developing country's standards, but organizers of the project believed when the local people worked together, they could accomplish amazing things.

The local organization poured its financial resources into staff members who lived within the poor communities, modeling Jesus's incarnational approach to ministry. The staff also facilitated the formation of small (twenty to thirty people) community action groups and gave those groups tools to better address their problems and analyze resources and potential solutions within their community.

By far, the majority of the self-help groups were comprised of women. They would meet weekly, discuss problems in their community, and come up with potential solutions. They would also contribute about twenty-five US cents per week out of their own pockets. If the group had twenty-five women (an average number), it would take in $6.25 per week.

Any member in good standing (who had participated and contributed financially each week) could propose to the group a project for funding. Initially, women wanted money to buy better seeds or healthier animals. Others wanted start-up capital to open a business, such as running a basic goods store out of their home. The SHG discussed, evaluated, and funded or rejected each project. The group also set up and monitored repayment terms for each idea.

The outside organization did not (and does not) infuse capital into the groups. It encourages the self-help groups to initiate and take ownership of every part of their work. The staff members facilitate the groups but leave the decisions to community members. Staff also helps with community-based projects, such as water systems and preschool education, but only as a part of a holistic community development process.

Within four years, the organization working in these communities had seen the formation of about 170 different self-help groups in a widespread area. Moreover, these groups had amassed a cash and asset balance of US $75,000. They began forming SHG affiliations, in which four or five SHGs would come together. They not only addressed individual projects but tackled larger, community-wide projects as well. The approach has been so successful that the organization facilitating the program is phasing out of this area and moving to another to begin the process again.

When I listened to the local ladies talk about their projects, I could hear the pride in their voices. I asked the local organization whether or not they were afraid to pull out of this community because the work might collapse. Its leader said, "It will not collapse. It is *their* program and *their* projects. They don't need us anymore."

The One Minute Manager Meets the Monkey

Over thirty years ago, someone recommended the book *The One Minute Manager Meets the Monkey* by Kenneth Blanchard, William Oncken Jr., and Hal Borrows. It was a part of the well-known One Minute Manager series of books. If you've never read *The One Minute Manager Meets the Monkey*, I encourage you to pick it up. It will only take you a couple of hours to read.

The book was written as a story with a lesson primarily for business leaders and managers in particular, in an attempt to help them see the value of not taking on their employees' responsibilities and tasks. In short, when an employee comes to their supervisor with a problem and the supervisor says, "I'll take care of that," that leader has effectively let a "monkey" leap off that employee's back onto their own. The book also gives practical tips on how to prevent and to deal with leaping monkeys.

When we as the church apply ministry-mission strategies to our community and kingdom engagement efforts, we need to be careful about accepting monkeys. In other words, we should not take problems off the shoulders of the community and place them squarely on our back. First, that approach is paternalistic. Second, it robs the local people of the chance to own and creatively address their problems. This not only affects their ability to solve the particular problem at hand, but it also drains the initiative and confidence of the community to address future problems. Taking away ownership of the problems in a community removes any possibility of reproducibility and sustainability.

On a visit to a poor, rural community, the leaders welcomed us outsiders with great fanfare and open arms. The chief quickly began telling us about all the problems the community faced. He painted a dire picture of little hope and no future. Honestly, it was a very compelling and true story, for the most part. Even in our brief time there, we could see that the community was among the poorest of the poor.

> Me: Thank you for sharing about your community. I am saddened to hear about all your problems. Can I ask you what you plan to do about them?

> The Chief (a little surprised by my question): The government doesn't help us. It doesn't have a lot of money, and it has a lot to do. Also, we are a long way from the capital, so we don't get much help.

> Me: I understand. But can I ask again? Do you have any plans to solve these problems?

> The Chief: We have some ideas, but we don't have many resources, so we don't think we can do much to solve these problems.

Me: I have a lot of experience in working with communities to help them think through their problems and come up with some solutions. Would you and your people be interested in hearing more?

The Chief: Maybe.

The good news is the chief and his community members were open to hearing our experiences. Within a few months, they had learned and applied some development principles and tools to address their problems. We facilitated the process, but they did the work. They evaluated what we were saying and chose to solve a problem that was critical in their eyes. The community came up with a solution and a plan to put the solution in place. Amazingly, the people had most of the resources they needed to solve that initial problem! This community's first project was so successful that it decided to address other problems, again utilizing the resources and skills they had. After four or five years, the community had begun to transform itself. It was hard to believe it was the same community we had started with.

Dos and Don'ts for Ministry Mission Projects

Christian anthropologist and missiologist Darrell Whiteman wrote a simple list of dos and don'ts for short-term mission trips. I've adapted it for those of us who want to utilize mercy-oriented missions strategies (with apologies to Dr. Whiteman).

1. Let local people determine your project. Your church can think of numerous ways to reach a community. However, start with the local people and their priorities.

2. Undertake sustainable projects. Don't create a project that depends on outside resources to keep going. The local people must be able to sustain it long term.

3. Don't create expectations that will burden future work. Most problems of poverty and disease are long-standing and have no simple solutions. Don't make promises you can't keep. Do what you can without setting up expectations about future accomplishments.

4. Don't patronize. Don't do anything for others that they can do for themselves.

Jesus as the Head, All of Us as the Body

At the start of this chapter, I quoted the apostle Paul who reminded us that there is only one head to the body: Jesus Christ. We as believers are the body. Everything and everyone are under Him, submitted to His Lordship. Each member of the body has a role to play, but that role isn't being the head of the body.

The passage applies to the church, but it also is a great picture of how churches and organizations should approach working with local communities in ministry projects. We are moved by the needs because of the compassion of Christ, our Head. We address needs because of our desire to show people God's plan for their lives and to make Christ known. And we enter a community with humility, knowing we are under His leadership and approach people and communities as potential coparticipants in the development process as well as the redemption He offers.

What We Learned

- Sustainability begins when local people take ownership of their problems and begin implementing their own solutions.
- If we have to turn over a project or work to locals, it isn't going to be sustainable (and it never was).
- Doing for others what they can do for themselves is not helpful to anyone in the long run.

PART 2

HOW TO DEVELOP A SUCCESSFUL MERCY-ORIENTED MISSIONS PROGRAM

TIPS FOR BUILDING AN INTENTIONAL MERCY-ORIENTED MISSIONS EFFORT

I lift my eyes toward the mountains. Where will my help come from?
My help comes from the Lord, the Maker of heaven and earth.

—Psalm 121:1–2

Cross-cultural mission work is difficult. Learning a new people group, their culture, their language, and finding ways to communicate the gospel in their cultural context is challenging, to say the least. Dealing with culture shock complicates our efforts. Why people do things that don't make sense to us can create confusion, misinterpretation, judgmental attitudes, and even anger. Cultural barriers can also lead us to reject (even if only subconsciously) the local people and culture.

Cross-cultural ministry projects can also be challenging. We as outsiders see the problem clearly, but the insiders don't seem to care or—worse—don't seem to recognize their problems at all. We give them animals to increase the breeding potential of their local stock, but they cook them for a meal at the wedding of one of their children. We provide a water well complete with a hand pump, but they seem unconcerned about repairing the pump when the handle breaks.

Cross-cultural ministry projects that lead to evangelism and discipleship can be difficult, especially for short-term teams in US churches where a long-term strategy is lacking. A group can go to a developing country for a week and put a new coat of paint on a school or orphanage. They can pull off a hands-on experience that highlights missions and helps church members feel good. However, investing time, people, and financial resources in a project that leads from good deed to sustainable evangelism, discipleship, and church planting is much more difficult. To see this happen in an unreached or hard-to-reach area of the world is rare indeed.

Before You Go, Ask These Six Questions

Whether you are looking to send out a short-term team or you are forming a long-term partnership that utilizes mercy-based missions, knowing the answers to the following questions will prove fruitful in the long run. Otherwise, you and your church members are likely to become frustrated by the lack of vision and sustainability.

1. Who are we? I know this sounds simple. The question is easy to answer when you're going to do a mercy-oriented missions project in a friendly or open country. Most of us can say, "I'm from _____ Church and we're here to _____." However, what do you say if your church is working in a more restricted area of the world or an area hostile to outsiders and Christians in particular? What if you're going to a country that has anticonversion laws for its citizens? What do you place on the immigration card in the space where it asks "purpose of visit" when you enter the country? Knowing who you are, publicly and privately, before you go is a critical first step. Missions groups need to create a short truthful statement (STS) that you can use anywhere you go. It is a truthful but brief statement that

keeps you, your mission, and your fellow team members in a defined box. Your basic STS might simply state that you are with a group that wants to help people gain access to clean drinking water and you are participating in a water development project. You may also need to have an expanded version of your STS to clarify anticipated questions from others. This expanded version would be a good place to talk about your faith as the reason why you are helping people with water needs.

When you create your STS, be careful of your terms. For instance, the word *Christian* can mean something entirely different in other cultures. Using the word could throw up red flags and barriers to deeper conversation. You might even be denied access to a country if you use this designation. As an alternative, you might describe yourself as a "follower of Jesus" or "person of deep faith" and see where the conversation goes.

2. What and who is our target? Your church or group needs to clarify who you want to reach and what you want to do. You also need to make clear whether you will intentionally share the gospel as a part of your work. For instance, someone in your church might want to organize a trip to paint an orphanage in Honduras. That's a good and noble activity. However, does painting help you accomplish the missions target of your church? It might be a good ministry project, but it doesn't help you proclaim the gospel. The what and who of ministry missions needs to be centered on people, their physical needs, and their eternal need to know Jesus.

Do we (the local church) want to target areas that have already evangelized and reached? Or have we prioritized the most unreached? When sharing about my missions experience through the years at churches in US, it is not uncommon to hear someone say, "Yeah, but we have a lot of lost people here at home." The point is well taken. We *do* have a lot of lost people in our own neighborhoods and towns. However, most (if not all) of those people have access to a church and have opportunity to hear the gospel multiple times and through multiple avenues. However, many people still live in areas of the world with little or no access to the gospel. Is one of these a priority for you and your church to focus on?

3. What are our goals and objectives? Many mission teams have not established specific goals and objectives before they go on a trip. When asked, they can come up with several good goals, but when asked if they have identified and named them beforehand, the people will usually say no. In the case of mercy-oriented mission projects, setting clear goals and objectives is critical to the project's success. It avoids the ambiguity of "We're just going over there to love on the people." Clear goals and objectives for a ministry project allows us to practice good stewardship. It helps us focus our efforts, time, and financial resources on things that we agree to as a strategic priority. For example, a church might say, "Our goal is to have one working water well by the time we leave, giving three hundred people access to clean drinking water."

A church or group also should make clear their spiritual goals and objectives. This is a necessity for the ministry project be a ministry *missions* project. A church might say, "Our goal is to share our testimony and the gospel with _____ (number) of people each day." As a church and sending body, we need to ensure that we train and equip our people to accomplish the goal.

4. What, where, and who is our appropriate entry point? I am not referring to the city or airport where your plane will land upon arrival. I am referring to the relationship or connection that facilitates access to your target people or area. This entry point or relationship may also become the long-term partner and sustainability component for the ongoing work after you are gone. This person should be a proven and trusted partner. (I'll discuss this later.) It could be a missionary you know well or a local believer or church leader you have found to be a potentially good implementing partner. In an underreached area, you may connect with a nonbeliever who helps facilitate your entry, implementation, and effectiveness of your ministry missions project.

Our organization encourages teams to look for people of peace and people of influence, especially in the beginning. Sometimes people of peace and influence are one in the same. Sometimes they are different altogether. A person of peace is someone God has prepared divinely to receive or be open to the gospel and will help facilitate gospel proclamation. Think of the woman at the well in John 4 as a good example of a person of peace. This Samaritan woman who had an encounter with Jesus heard the truth of who Jesus was, believed in Him, and told all her friends and family.

A person of influence is also divinely appointed and will facilitate entry into a community or target area, but they may never become a follower of Christ. For some reason, they are happy to help a group implement the beneficial project in a community and are generally sympathetic with a church's beliefs. Perhaps because they want the best for their community, they see value in what we Westerners do and thus help facilitate a project's success. In many countries, persons of influence have helped our organization with government approvals or permissions, relationships in local communities, and even teaching and promoting the things a group is doing to help them. Even though we grow closer and share life and the gospel, many of these partners still choose not to become Christ followers despite hearing and understanding the message. We commit these relationships to prayer and continue in the work alongside them, yearning and hoping for the day they come to faith. In some cases, we don't see their conversion, but God uses them to facilitate the ministry project and gospel proclamation to their people.

5. What are our skills, gifts, and abilities as well as our limitations? Believers don't transform into superheroes when we step off the plane. We're the same people who left own home countries, with the same skills sets and character flaws we had back in the US. That's why it's important to know team members' abilities and limitations before we leave.

I pride myself on being a handyman, the proverbial jack-of-all-trades, master-of-none. I enjoy building things and working with my hands. However, I don't possess all the skills necessary to construct a hospital. I can use my skills, but I also need to rely on the more advanced skills of others. The gifts of the whole team need to be taken into consideration.

Too often, we outsiders tend to overlook the skills and knowledge of the local people. A good team aiming to engage in a ministry missions project acknowledges what they can and cannot do before the project begins. In most cases, the local people possess the gifts and skills necessary to complete the work. And such involvement gives the people ownership, which is a primary goal of any successful project.

6. How do we know when we are successful and when we are finished with our work? This question ties directly to the goals and objectives a church establishes before it begins a project. Clear objectives and expectations at the outset make it easier to recognize when our job is done. I have found that most churches don't like to talk about ending their mission projects. It is uncomfortable. Or churches simply set an arbitrary end date (e.g., three to five years) based upon previous experiences or because they can't keep their people interested past this time frame.

Declaring a project complete doesn't mean every problem is solved or everyone in the target area knows Jesus. It means you have reached your goals, empowered local groups to carry on the work, and need to exit in order for them to flourish and not be hindered by your continued presence.

The exit strategy criteria should be set early on, but it can (and needs to) be adjusted based upon actual experiences in the field. This strategy needs to be communicated not only with your church and teams but also with those you are going to help. To establish the exit criteria, start with an end point in mind that allows you to implement mercy-oriented work well and see people and communities transformed by the gospel. You want to see the people grow in their love for God, for their neighbors, and for themselves (Matthew 22:36–40). Ultimately, you want to see the local believers take up the task of sharing Christ in their community, their nation, and to the uttermost parts of the world.

Ten Principles to Consider as You Go

As you and your church venture into mercy-oriented ministry projects as a missional strategy, consider some of the principles addressed in this book. Keeping them in mind will make your efforts more effective and will give you a metric to measure whether or not you are approaching your next missions project on a solid foundation.

1. Seek to understand before being understood. This principle from chapter 8 bears repeating here. It is foundational not to just mercy-oriented missions but all mission endeavors, and it is why long-term missionaries take time to learn language and culture. Communicating effectively in another language and from another worldview is not easy, and it can oftentimes be misinterpreted.

From a Western US mindset, we are some of the worst offenders when it comes to interpreting things from our own culture and perspective. We are problem solvers and want to fix things. Combined with our desire for immediate and quick results, our lack of understanding can lead to hasty and unhealthy solutions in our cross-cultural work.

The first law of bioethics in medicine is "First, do no harm." If there is a golden rule in mercy-oriented missions, it simply this: first, seek to understand. People do what they do for a reason. There is logic behind how they solve their everyday problems. It may not make sense to us initially as outsiders, but we don't possess all the facts that would allow us to evaluate and judge people's actions fairly. This is why it is important to be quick to listen and slow to interject our thoughts.

The way people do things is not perfect. But it is *their* way. Understanding the why behind the what is a key in helping them discover better ways to improve upon their existing practices. We outsiders need to learn from them, help them build on their good practices, and (hopefully) improve their future decisions.

2. Check your ethnocentrism, value judgments, and stereotypes at the door. As stated in chapter 2, how we see people affects the way we treat them. When we outsiders look at a family living in poverty in a developing country and say, "They are poor because _____ " (fill in the blank), we have made a value judgment based our understanding and perception, which may be completely inaccurate.

Poverty, hunger, and underdevelopment are highly complex issues and require complex solutions. The suffering stemming from these issues is beyond our control or ability to fix. Thus, we gravitate to one or two people, families, or small communities to do *something* to make a difference. We think if people have better animals, seeds, income, etc., they will have better lives. We implement our poverty alleviation projects, like feeding programs, job-skills training, or better farming methods, hoping the infusion of solutions will eliminate their problems.

We believe if they learn how to be hard workers (like us), they can pull themselves out of poverty. We think they have missed opportunities because they don't have the resources we have, so we supply them new things. We believe new technology solves a problem and gets them out of impoverishment. We believe in some mystical key to solve their problems, and our job is to help them find it.

Here is that not-so-secret key: the people themselves. The solution to systemic problems does not come from what we offer from the outside. People working together to improve themselves, their families, and their communities is the solution to sustainable development. Outsiders like us can help, but the local people need to catch the vision in order to move forward in development. Our resources can help, but the inside resources must drive the development because we cannot remain involved indefinitely.

And at a deeper level, people working together to create change and experience a relationship with God are the foundation of sustainable and transformational development. Created in the image of God, they live in community as God planned with Him as the head, and they come together to see "His kingdom come, His will be done, on earth as it is in heaven."

3. Embrace your own brokenness and dependency on God. When we look at people and communities struggling in poverty and underdevelopment, we think they are broken—and they are. But you and I are broken people as well. We are *all* part of a broken, fallen race of humanity.

People in undeveloped countries are broken (like us), but they are not defective. They face significant needs, but they are happy and love their families just like you and I do. They need a Savior, but that is not our role. They possess amazing talents, abilities, and skills we cannot see from the outside.

Those of us from affluent countries tend to forget we are totally dependent on God. We depend on Him for every breath we take. We depend on Him for every good gift. Ironically, the goodness and the blessings of God can (and do) lead us to take our eyes off God. Then we are prone to approach our missions work in an unhealthy mindset of "us" who have it all together going to help "them" who are in some way less than we are.

Our goal in mercy-oriented missions is not to create mirror versions of ourselves and provide others with all the things we do. Our goal is to help people see Jesus so they can be transformed by His amazing mercy and grace, like we are being transformed.

4. Keep in mind the community's history. Most church members involved in mercy-oriented mission endeavors have a punctiliar understanding of the people and communities they want to help. They have entered that group at a particular time and place, and they base their understanding of the people on what they have seen, heard, and experienced in that moment int time. In some cases, they go back to the same people, place, and community at the same time every year, reinforcing that limited perspective.

For example, if you were to visit the southern Philippines during the month of February, you might conclude the land was dry and unfit for any crops to grow. You would also note the respiratory problems related to the constant blowing dust. As an outsider, you might conclude that water for agriculture production was a huge problem and that the people need solutions to arid land cropping.

The truth is the area *does* have a pronounced dry season, but it only lasts for two or three months. The rest of the year, the area has ample (even surplus) rainfall, which allows for two crops of rice per year in the lowlands and two crops of maize (corn) in the uplands. But because you saw this place at a particular point in time and under a particular set of circumstances, it would be easy to make wrong assumptions.

While that is an oversimplified example, it represents the problem of a limited perspective. We outsiders need to understand that the people and communities we are serving have survived for centuries before we got there, and they will likely survive for centuries after we leave (if the Lord tarries). Therefore, they must be doing something right. They must have knowledge and expertise that you and I don't have.

I am not suggesting a community doesn't have needs, dreams, and goals for their betterment. However, I am suggesting that we should be careful about interjecting our views, interpretations, and thoughts without understanding a group's history and context.

5. Recognize that risk looks different to people in developing countries. We as outsiders need to understand risk from the point of view of those with whom we are trying to do ministry missions. Most of us have accepted an axiom that isn't always true. "People are afraid of change." We apply this to the people and communities we have worked with in mercy-oriented mission projects.

"They won't adopt our ideas because they are afraid to change their ways."

"Why are these people so slow to change? Don't they know what is good for them?"

"It's frustrating to work with these people. They are so slow in doing anything new!"

My experience is that people are not resistant to change; they are concerned about what's at stake if they attempt an outsider's new idea.

Poverty systems are stable but fragile. Unlike you and your church members who come from affluent societies in which the basics of life (food, water, income, healthcare, etc.) are a mere afterthought, impoverished people and communities can lose what little they have with even the smallest of changes.

For a US farmer to try a new seed variety or farming technique, it would not be a big risk. If it failed, that farmer could absorb the loss and, in most cases, find government funding or use private insurance to fall back on. On the other hand, a farmer in a developing country trying a new seed variety or farming technique could risk the viability of his entire family. If the new venture failed, his children might drop out of school. Or worse, the farmer might lose a whole cropping season and be driven deeper into poverty and hunger.

A person who makes $30,000 USD per year and lives in a country with safety nets like social security and secure bank loans cannot compare their concerns and decision-making process to someone who lives on a fraction of those resources with no safety net. Losing money can cause hardship for the Westerner, but they still have options if the risk doesn't earn a reward. On the other hand, the loss of a few dollars for a person or family in a developing country can be life-threatening.

I remember one young farmer in a rural, mountainous area of the Philippines whose family almost came to ruin because he developed a hernia from lifting and hauling sacks of corn to the market. He couldn't work for a season and it affected his children's education, the income of the family, and their ability to feed themselves. Thankfully, he was able to get surgery and eventually went back to work. If someone in the US suffered the same ailment, the setback would be inconvenient but not on the same scale as the Filipino farmer. We outsiders cannot judge those in developing countries for being slow to accept change or take a risk.

6. Participate in a long-term strategy. Since people and communities exist and develop at their own pace, and since many are slow to change because of the inherit risk involved, your mercy-oriented missions efforts need to be a part of a long-term strategy.

On average, you and your church will be involved in a particular area with a particular ministry for three to five years. If possible, the church will make one or two short-term trips to the area each year. A lot happens in the community during the other fifty weeks when your mission team is not on the ground. Furthermore, a lot will happen after you leave and look for another area to work. Tying your short-term work to an on-the-ground, long-term strategy is a smart approach if you want to maximize your effectiveness.

That long-term strategy could involve connecting with a career missionary you know and can trust. This person would be invested in the local community, understand its language and culture, prepare for your arrival and work with your team while you are there, and follow up on the ministry results that occurred during your time in the community.

The long-term strategy could also involve a local partner, such as a church or community. You will need to agree on the scope of your work, goals for your team, and the expectations on both sides. This will pave the way for the mutual impact on the community, and it will empower the local partner for future work.

Whether you work with a missionary or local church in the target area, I would encourage you to see your church as a contributor to the long-term strategy and efforts of your partner on the field. You bring your ideas, gifts, and passion, all of which are important. But since your partner will be invested in the work on a permanent basis, you need to find ways to enhance *their* plans, work, and effectiveness in the target area instead of focusing on your own.

7. Choose to work with trusted partners. This begs the question "What is a trusted partner?" This is a person or group you and your church can partner with because you have a high level of trust in them. They will have a proven track record of doing sound theological and missiological work. They utilize good community development and biblical principles in meeting others' needs. And they have a heart for and track record of making disciples.

I am not going to provide a checklist defining a trusted partner. My criteria may be a bit different from yours. However, I will offer some advice.

- Pray about every potential new partnership. Ask God for wisdom and discernment through His Holy Spirit.
- Realize that not everyone you meet is a good partner for your church's missions efforts. A pastor from overseas who sends you a random friend request over social media with an appeal for help may not be the best potential partner.
- Work through trusted and reputable mission-minded organizations that can guide you to good partners on the field.
- Look for evidence-based results from your potential partner's work, and evaluate how well they work among the people in the target communities.
- Early on, make sure you are ideologically and theologically compatible. An African proverb I've heard goes something like this: "If you want to go fast, go alone. If you want to go far, go together." I would add, "If you want to see continued ministry results long after you're gone, work with a trusted partner."

8. Set realistic expectations. There are no quick fixes to the problems of the world. Such systemic and dramatic change takes time. Our Band-Aid solutions rarely yield any appreciable change. Not only are community members dealing with multiple problems—lack of seeds, poor water quality, limited access to health care options, etc.—but they also contend with outside influences and forces that contribute to the success or failure of sustainable development.

For example, bad or corrupt government at a national level can seriously impact communities on the local level. International finance, foreign political powers, and selfish decisions by politicians and regimes can literally devastate local economies. Climate change and shifting weather patterns can hamper a community's ability to grow and produce food. Wars and armed conflicts can cause huge geographical shifts in populations, availability of goods, and the security of a people. Deeply held and centuries-long religious restrictions and cultural practices influence how people view their situations and their options for a better life. These huge and outside forces shape the development or underdevelopment of a particular people or area.

This reality should not discourage us from wanting to help people through mercy-oriented mission efforts. However, these forces and struggles people face should lead us to be more realistic about our expectations for anticipated change. Slowing down and seeking to understand the political, social, religious, and economic structure of a community will lead us to better sustainable and effective solutions to their problems. There are multiple factors outside a community's control, but we can help the people see and address the problems they *can* control, while also maintaining a spirit of humility and respect.

Thankfully, we believers are not called to solve the world's problems. We are called to participate in the lives of others to ease their suffering where we can and to point them to the One who can bring about ultimate and lasting peace.

9. Work for reproducible change. A good missions or church-planting strategy focuses on reproducibility. We as believers want people who come to faith to reproduce their faith in the lives of others God puts in their paths. We want people who become disciples of Christ to disciple others. We want churches that are planted to grow and plant other churches.

This principle of reproducibility applies in our mercy-oriented mission efforts as well. We want to build structures and programs that the local people can sustain and reproduce on their own. In some instances, such as a major disaster event, we outsiders provide the resources and labor to carry out a project. However, mercy-oriented ministries should focus on the tasks a local community can carry out and later multiply in other areas, creating a multiplying ripple effect in an area and even a country.

Medical and health care clinics run by outside organizations should incorporate strategies and skills to enhance the local health providers' services and allow them to grow in self-sufficiency.

Water development programs providing clean wells, water filtration methods, or better water quality need to give increased knowledge, skill, and capacities to local communities. This will allow them to solve their water issues now and in the future.

New and improved agriculture methods and techniques should be based on and improve on existing practices local people already know and lead toward small but incremental changes the people can maintain and expand on.

Job skills training and microbusiness initiatives work best when they incorporate the knowledge and resources of the local people from the very beginning. They know far better what skills and businesses will thrive in their corner of the world.

When we work from our outsider perspective and don't take in account the local people and their ideas, we run the risk of making it *our* program, *our* ideas, and *our* solutions. This inevitably leads to methods and projects that cannot be reproduced. The project may work for a time, but it will prove ineffective once outsiders leave. People in developing countries can accomplish more amazing and longer-lasting results than what we outsiders can imagine from our skewed and privileged perspective.

10. Make intentional efforts toward kingdom impact. It should go without saying, but I want to make sure this last point is clear: effective mercy-oriented mission projects incorporate the gospel, evangelism, discipleship, and church planting in all its humanitarian efforts. We must be intentional about making Christ known as we care for the hurting. We cannot assume people will learn about Christ by our actions and good deeds.

Good deeds and good actions naturally flow out from the love of Christ in us. However, believers should not neglect the clear proclamation of the gospel. "So faith comes from what is heard, and what is heard comes through the message about Christ" (Romans 10:17).

- Before you go, be willing to ask yourself some hard questions.
- As you go, remember the principles of good development work.
- When you go, go in prayer, humility, and maintaining a learning posture that God is already at work.

THREE KEYS TO MEASURING SUCCESS IN MERCY-ORIENTED MISSIONS: INTERNAL, EXTERNAL, AND ETERNAL INDICATORS

Remember the earlier days when, after you had been enlightened,
you endured a hard struggle with sufferings. Sometimes you
were publicly exposed to taunts and afflictions, and at other
times you were companions of those who were treated that way.
For you sympathized with the prisoners and accepted with joy
the confiscation of your possessions, because you know that
you yourselves have a better and enduring possession.

—Hebrews 10:32–34

So how do we know if the well we dug in Africa was a successful project? Or if the feeding program for underprivileged children *really* made a difference? These questions highlight the need for tangible indicators and measurement criteria to help evaluate our work.

In a recent conversation at a conference, I talked with a group that had been conducting medical work in a foreign country for decades. They were proud of their work and cited the thousands of patients treated, the number of medical mission trips their church had taken, and the satisfaction they felt for all the good they had done through the years. Yet they were struggling. They had come to a crossroads and were beginning to question the impact they were having. They were wrestling with whether they needed to back out of this particular ministry and look for other places in the world to work.

Me: How long has your church been providing health care services in this place?

Them: For almost two decades.

Me: And you've seen good results?

Them: Oh yes! We have been able to treat and help thousands of people. A small building serves as a clinic, a local staff does everything we ask, and we have developed a good reputation in the community.

Me: How much is the local community contributing to the finances and operation of this program?

Them: None, really. They are so poor and we're not sure they could.

Me: Have you helped them [the local staff] think of ways to generate income and bear a part of the budget through their own resources?

Them: Oh no. They are busy serving the community.

Me: Do the patients who come to the clinic pay anything for their treatment?

Them: Not really. It is a ministry.

Me: Have you attempted to tap their government and other local resources [such as local nongovernment organizations] for funding and support?

Them: Not really. We were told that those organizations are corrupt, so we should not work with them.

Me: So what is it you are asking me to help you with?

Them: Our church is questioning what to do. We have been working with this particular ministry for several years, and we are trying phase out and move on to other things. But we are afraid that if we stop funding this ministry, it will cease to exist. We will have wasted twenty years of work, and the local people will have no access to health care services.

Me: Okay, here's my next question, and it's a hard one. Have you talked to your local national partner team and told them all of this—your plans, your expectations, your dreams for the future?

Them: Well, no, not really.

Three Categories of Measuring Success in Your Mercy-Oriented Ministry

I would like to propose the following three levels or categories for measuring success (or lack thereof) in any mercy-oriented missions effort:

- the internal
- the external
- the eternal

As outsiders, we can measure the visible results, such as how many water wells were dug, how many hungry people were fed, or how many people were treated in our medical clinics. These physical indicators are the easiest numbers to measure, and they are the ones we use to prepare nice reports to share with our donors and supporters.

Even though important, these pure numbers don't tell the deeper story. What *really* happened in the lives of the people and the community because of our project? It helped people, but did it change them and make them better for the future? If so, how do we recognize and measure that change?

These three areas (internal, external, and eternal) help us gain a complete picture of the impact of our efforts when we feed the hungry, give water to the thirsty, and care for the sick. We should be in conversation with the local community members to determine the internal indicators. We ask ourselves about the external indicators as outside development workers. And we should be praying and constantly seeking God in what He is doing among the people. Those are the eternal indicators.

1. Internal indicators. What happens in the hearts and lives of those we are called to work with inside the target community? What changes have we seen that will enable the people to better address their immediate and future needs long after we outsiders are gone? The local people should measure these changes. We can facilitate the assessment of their progress and growth, but the evaluation belongs to them.

We as outsiders rejoice when we see people gain access to clean water. We are happy when they get better roads or better access to health care. But what are the intangible or internal measurements that indicate a community is developing in a way that allows it to grow and become a fully productive, whole kingdom community? In my experience, the following five internal indicators demonstrate development in a community:

A. *Capabilities* – What new abilities, skills, and knowledge have the members of the community learned or gained in order to solve their local problems? These could be process-oriented skills, or they could be practical skills, such as increased knowledge in health care, agriculture, and water development. The skills could also be business related, such as simple bookkeeping, marketing, and production of a local product. Long before we arrive in a community, it has already acquired existing skills for survival and development. It wouldn't still be in existence if it didn't. However, we as outsiders want to know what new abilities the people have accrued as they have implemented their initial development projects. Will these skills allow the people to begin to address more challenging and even larger developmental issues in their community? Since our incursion into their lives, are they now better off in terms of abilities to move forward in development when we outsiders are not there anymore?

B. *Capacities* – How has the community increased its capacity to address not only immediate needs but also long-term, larger needs in the future? Maybe the people installed a new water system in their community as a first-step development project. But besides providing clean water, what new capacities developed? How were their existing capacities expanded to address even larger, more complex problems for the future? Did the community develop new networks with government agencies or nongovernment groups? Did it discover untapped interior resources as well as those outside the community? Did its potential for problem solving expand to address greater challenges? Did the people gain a new process or tools to help them break down complex problems into bite-sized, implementable steps leading to practical, local, sustainable solutions? Again, the community members must take the lead in evaluating its growth. Outsiders cannot adequately assess that.

C. *Community* – A chief principle of community development is to start with a group of people with a common interest or goal, so one of the key internal measurements of success would naturally be how the people grew as a community as a result of the work they did together. The people solved the problem of obtaining clean water for the members of the community, but how did they do this in a way that increased their caring and love for one another? How did the project affect the people who live in close relationship with one another? Did it make them better and stronger together, or did it cause strife, jealousy, and discord?

One of the reasons we outsiders focus on how a community implemented a particular project is because stronger communities are poised for better development for the future. People working together in good relationships with one another is as important as learning a better way to raise chickens, building an improved road, or starting a micro-enterprise project. From a development worker's viewpoint, we should constantly be aware of and evaluating what happens in the lives of people, rather than how many projects they implement.

D. *Confidence* – A common consequence of systemic poverty is that people and communities feel hopeless. They think they cannot do much to change their future. This is sometimes described as the poverty trap, and it is created by a lack of access to capital, services, and opportunities to grow. Poverty, especially generational poverty, can begin to erode the confidence and ability of people and communities to see a way out. Many times, this attitude results in a fatalistic acceptance of a substandard way of life. One of the intangible but important measurements of effective community development is how the community's image of itself begins to enlarge and how the members of the community begin to experience success and a newfound confidence. They begin to believe they can do something about their situations, not only today but for the future. When a community comes together, when capabilities and capacities expand, and when small projects bring about positive change, the people gain new confidence in being able change their lives. When people working together begin to experience success, it can make all the difference in their outlook and willingness to move forward in the development process.

E. Christlikeness – Think of this measurement as a community character check. We know that true Christlikeness can only be expressed through a regenerated heart filled with the Holy Spirit. However, any movement toward Christlikeness, such as a community living by biblical values and seeking justice and fairness for the whole community, can lead to fertile ground for making Christ's name known.

Biblical principles of truth, justice, mercy, and good relationships are universal. When we outsiders can see a community living out these principles, even without regenerated hearts, we see an increased potential for future development and gospel impact. Communities being introduced to kingdom values is like plowing the ground before sowing the seeds. The plowing cultivates the ground so the seed can be received to a good seed bed, increase the possibility of sprouting, and eventual grow to a full crop. Our ultimate goal and heart in mercy-oriented missions is to see God's kingdom come and His will be done in the community through a right relationship and worship of Jesus. But our preparation oftentimes begins with simple concepts of neighbors loving one another, showing mercy, and living justly together.

Questions a Community Can Ask to Evaluate Internal Development

- What new skills or abilities has the community learned since entering the community development process?
- What are some ways the community has improved upon its traditional practices?
- Is the community better off today than it was two years ago? Why?
- Have you formed any partnerships with outside organizations or groups to help develop your community? If so, with whom? What benefit does this bring to your community?
- Is your community better as a unit since you started the development process?

- How do your neighbors help one another and show support for one another?
- How to you feel about the future development potential of your community?
- On a scale of one to ten, with ten being the best score, how do you rate your community's ability to solve the problems it faces?
- Have you seen a positive change in the way community members treat each other? If so, how?
- Is your community one in which people would be interested in living? Why or why not?

2. External indicators. This is a measurement of our ourselves about ourselves and our programs. What do our programs cause in the community? This is not about numbers (wells built, farms helped, etc.), but rather the way the people and community as a whole are changed because it interacted with us. It is an assessment of how well we (outsiders) helped people move forward in development and whether or not our methods lined up with good development principles. This is why we label these as external measurements. It is more about how we work with the community as opposed to what happens in the community itself.

- Participation – Are our efforts in a community, the way we work and interact with them, truly participatory? Are we involving the local community in all aspects of the development process? Whose development program is it? Whose problems are being addressed? Whose solutions are being implemented? Do the local people own and drive the community development process they are undergoing, or is it dependent on us the outsiders? Who is evaluating the success or failure: the insiders or the outsiders? Participation implies action on the part of both the outsiders (the development workers) and the insiders (the community). A healthy indicator of good development is growing involvement of the local community over time, while our involvement from the outside diminishes over time.

- Sustainability – Are our efforts to help the community sustainable? Have we adequately empowered local people in the development process, or have we created a process that depends on outsiders to continue? Sustainability is a common buzzword, but it is also important in measuring development. A simple test is observing what happens in the community after one or two development cycles in which the community has implemented a particular solution to a problem. Are the people now addressing other outstanding problems largely on their own initiative, or are they still looking to outsiders to lead and solve their problems for them?

- Transformation – Is true transformation taking place in the community due to our efforts? Improvements are being made, such as better roads, clean water, and more income, but are there also improvements in the way the community works together and treats each other? Are more biblical values being embraced because of our interaction with the people? Are more people hearing the truth about God? Is there more gospel access because of our involvement? Are lives being transformed as only God's Word and Spirit can do? We as outsiders cannot adequately measure the work of God based on behavior alone, but we can measure how well we have modeled Christ in word and deed.

Questions to Help Us Determine Our Effectiveness as External Influencers

- Who is responsible for the good development in the community where we work?
- Do you think your community will continue developing after outside organizations are gone?

- Which word best describes the community and its role in the development process: participant or recipient?
- If all outside organizations and groups left the community today, would it continue to develop?
- What skills and knowledge have you gained from the community you served?
- Is the community better today than it was before development workers came in?
- What are some positive things that you now see in the community that you didn't see before? What are some of the negative things?

3. Eternal. This is our final indicator of good development and our ultimate goal of working with those in need. Where is the kingdom impact for the local people and community? This is a measurement of the big picture and eternal impact of our efforts. People obtained clean water, more food, better health, and other elements important for their day-to-day living and welfare, but was their eternity impacted by what we did? Was it holistic? Did our work honor God and proclaim Him as Lord and Savior?

Instead of me providing questions for you to ask the community regarding eternal impact, let me relate a story that illustrates a total impact of a mercy-oriented ministry.

A Picture of a Transformed Community

I recently saw a transformed community. Three years ago, an earthquake had rocked the town. It destroyed homes. It buried livestock under collapsed stone barns. It took out the town's water system and took away loved ones. Everyone in the community grieved. Life as they had known it was gone.

Enter a well-trained community development worker. He sat with the leaders, often in silence. Eventually, they opened up and poured out their hearts. They talked about rebuilding their future.

Hope began to break through as the community came together. They couldn't bring back their loved ones, but they could bring back their community from chaos, despair, and hopelessness.

Fast-forward to today. The people have rebuilt their homes, due in part to the community development worker and their organization, but mostly due to government grants awarded to the community because it had organized, taken charge, and sought out those funds.

The community development worker led the community to implement a new and improved water system. He also helped with animal and seed dispersals to jump-start the farmers' work. Today, every home has a vegetable garden and animal project, and most homes have running water.

The best sign of transformation? A small church with a handful of people has grown to a group of over 150 worshipping together. Many in the community who had persecuted the handful of believers have since become faithful members of the local body. The community had witnessed the compassion and love of the church, and it was moved by what the followers of Jesus had done for them. Not only is the church healthy and growing, but it has also started another group in a neighboring village.

The gospel was shared in love—in word and in deed. Hope was demonstrated in a tangible way, and truth was spoken. Internally, confidence was restored in the community. Capacities and capabilities were expanded. Community ties and relationships were renewed and strengthened. And Christlikeness was demonstrated by the handful of believers to the rest of the suffering community, and its people began to exhibit that Christlike spirit. Today, the community not only has clean water, rebuilt homes, and productive farms but also a sense of purpose meaning that is unmistakable as you enter their community. People are productive in their work, children are going to school, and life is good today.

Externally, the development workers used good, participatory methods for development in this particular community. They sat with the community leaders in their grief until they were ready to begin to rebuild their lives and their community. Workers listened and acted on the community's priorities as they began to help people restore their farms and lives to productivity. The process of recovery and restoration remained with the community, allowing local ownership of not only the problems but also the solutions.

Eternally, the kingdom impact was huge. From an initial small handful of believers meeting together, the church has grown much larger. It has begun outreach in a neighboring area that saw the development and change as a testimony to the goodness of God. Believers have grown from a group persecuted and shunned by the community to a growing, vital part of the community that demonstrates and boldly proclaims the message of hope in Christ.

What We Learned

- What happens internally in the lives and hearts of those we work with is more important than what happens to them externally.
- How we outsiders approach our work with a community highly influences whether or not the results will be sustainable in the long-term.
- We work for the development of a community in the present moment, but we also recognize the eternal weight of our work in the people and community.

SO DO YOU REALLY WANT TO DIG A WELL IN AFRICA?

THE HEART OF MERCY-ORIENTED MISSIONS

As He approached Jericho, a blind man was sitting by the road begging.
Hearing a crowd passing by, he inquired what was happening.
"Jesus of Nazareth is passing by," they told him.
So he called out, "Jesus, Son of David, have mercy on me!"
Then those in front told him to keep quiet, but he kept crying
out all the more, "Son of David, have mercy on me!"
Jesus stopped and commanded that he be brought to Him. When he
came closer, he asked him, "What do you want Me to do for you?"
"Lord," he said, "I want to see."
"Receive your sight." Jesus told him. "Your faith has saved you."
Instantly he could see, and he began to follow Him, glorifying
God. All the people, when they saw it, gave praise to God.

—Luke 18:35–43

This is an interesting story. It is the healing of a blind man who sat beside the road begging for his daily bread. From the parallel story in Mark's account, we know this blind man's name was Bartimaeus.

Bartimaeus hears the sound of a crowd. He asks those passing by what all the commotion is about. When the people tell him Jesus of Nazareth is passing by, his heart likely leaps for joy. Surely Bartimaeus had heard about Jesus, the great teacher. Jesus was also a healer and worker of miracles. He had made the lame walk. He had restored hearing to the deaf. He had cast out demons. He had even has raised the dead. But the best thing to Bartimaeus? He had given sight to the blind.

So Bartimaeus calls out to Jesus for mercy. "Jesus, Son of David, have mercy on me!" (v. 38).

In the midst of the pressing crowd, Jesus hears the call for mercy. Never mind the throng of people surrounding Jesus. Never mind them pressing in to see Him and possibly ask for something they needed. Never mind that Jesus had already set His face toward Jerusalem and was on the road to the cross. Jesus hears Bartimaeus's cry for mercy.

And Jesus stops. Jesus calls the man to Himself and asks him this simple yet compassionate question: "What do you want Me to do for you?" (v. 41).

Jesus asked, and Jesus listened. Jesus didn't presume to know what Bartimaeus wanted. Of course, Jesus knew what he needed and wanted because He was God incarnate. And it was pretty obvious, even to those who surrounded Jesus, that this blind man was asking for mercy. He wanted his sight restored.

Yet Jesus asks a question and gives dignity to Bartimaeus by allowing him to voice the deepest needs of his heart. "Lord, I want to see" (v. 41).

This is more than a self-serving request by Bartimaeus. It is a faith response to who Jesus is and what He can do. We know this because Jesus proclaims, "Receive your sight; your faith has saved you" (v. 42).

The result? Bartimaeus is healed. He recovers his sight immediately. He believes and follows Jesus, giving glory to God. And amazingly, when those looking on see this happen, they also give praise and honor to God (v. 43).

That morning, Jesus didn't set out on the road to Jerusalem to dig a well. Or even to heal a blind man. He was on a mission to make the kingdom of God known. That would ultimately be accomplished by death on a cross and resurrection by the power of the Father. All of this would occur in a few short days after his encounter with Bartimaeus. The lesson here is twofold.

1. Jesus went about doing good (Acts 10:38). He was full of power and of the Spirit. He was full of truth. Yet He also had compassion for people who had physical and spiritual needs. He had compassion for the whole person. There was no separation of proclaiming and demonstrating the love of God. Both were essential and both led to the same message: the kingdom of God has come among you. The kingdom was fully manifested in the person and work of Christ.

2. True mercy in God's kingdom always focuses on the good of human beings and the glory of God. Bartimaeus received his sight. That was for the good of Bartimaeus. But as good as this was, it was a true act of mercy because God was glorified. Bartimaeus believed. Bartimaeus followed. Bartimaeus glorified God for His goodness. When they saw what happened, even the onlookers gave praise and glory to God.

First and foremost, mercy ministries and mercy-oriented missions focus on the good of people—addressing their most deeply felt needs—and ultimately on the glory of God.

The Greatest Act of Mercy Ever: Our Motivation

So why do we even care about mercy-oriented missions? Isn't it easier to simply focus on evangelism and disciple-making? After all, isn't that the core task of missions? My answer is yes and no. I believe we are called to do mercy-oriented missions for four reasons.

1. The love of Christ compels us. As regenerated followers of Jesus Christ, the Spirit of Christ lives in us. His heart of compassion for a

world in need compels us to show mercy as we have been shown mercy. Christ embodied the perfect mercy focus of loving and ministering to people where they hurt yet always focused on eternity. He Himself is the greatest revelation of word and deed.

2. The needs of people move us. As fellow human beings, our hearts are disturbed when we see disasters and chronic issues, such as hunger and poverty. The struggle and suffering of people due to some calamity in their lives moves us in our innermost being. Even nonbelievers have their hearts stirred when they see the devastation of a killer earthquake or massive tsunami on the evening news. People in need speaks to the deepest part of our soul because we are reminded of the fragility of our own lives in the suffering of others.

3. The Word of God commands us. God tells us to care for the poor. Yes, especially those within the household of faith, but not to the exclusion of non-believers. One measurement of our walk with Christ is the way we the treat and deal with others, especially the poor and disenfranchised.

4. The desire to make Christ known inspires us. We believe that acts of compassion and mercy can be visible demonstrations of the love of God. Moreover, they become avenues for sharing the truth of Christ, which gives people freedom for eternity.

What is the greatest act of mercy in all of history? It is not our efforts at doing good, no matter how unselfish our intentions or how worthy our actions. It is not giving clean water and better health care to people in need. It is not helping people and communities recover from disasters or climb out of poverty. *The greatest act of mercy in all of history took place when God sent His Son Jesus to save an undeserving world.* And that is our ultimate motivation for showing mercy—because God has shown great mercy to us.

What is the greatest expression of mercy that you or I can extend to anyone? It is simply to proclaim to them, "Be reconciled to God" (2

Corinthians 5:20). John Piper has simply put it this way, saying, "We care about all suffering, especially eternal suffering."

Three Key Concluding Questions

Here are some final questions and thoughts in light of what you have read in the previous pages:

1. Do you really want to dig a well or *something* else? You can substitute "dig a well" with "build an orphanage," "run a clinic," "start a food pantry," or any number of other ministries. The question is about the reason we want to do ministry and missions. What is the ultimate goal in what you want to do? Many who are gifted and called to do mercy-oriented missions criticize evangelists and disciple-makers for their lack of ministry to the whole person. But in all honestly, those who are mercy oriented and gifted oftentimes struggle to keep a focus on gospel proclamation and eternal outcomes. The challenge in mercy-oriented missions is to remain committed to proclaiming the kingdom in the midst of ministry efforts. We as believers want to give clean water to the thirsty, food to the hungry, and health care to the sick, but our overarching motivation must lie within in the framework of eternity and proclaiming the kingdom of God.

2. Do you really want to dig a well in Africa or *somewhere* else? I have nothing against Africa (or anywhere else for that matter). However, God may not be leading you to Africa. In missions, churches gravitate toward familiar and convenient places. As a result, they wind up doing missions in areas that are easily accessible (close to the US and/or easy to travel to), friendly to outsiders (the people speak English), and places the church has been before. We gravitate toward sites where we can travel relatively easily, enjoy a great experience, get good stories, and return every summer like a well-oiled machine.

The question is this: are we serious about missions and making Christ known to *unreached* people? If your passion is to dig a well, why not ask if God wants you to dig one in an unreached and unchurched area of the world? Billions of people live in underserved areas of the world. What if God wants to use your well to not only bring water to a thirsty community but also to bring light to the spiritually darkest areas?

3. Do the people you're going to work with even *want* a well? Maybe your passion is clean water. Or maybe it is feeding hungry people. Or perhaps it is taking care of orphans. For the sake of the gospel, would you be willing to consider a project that isn't your personal passion? Too often, we as churches look at missions and our mission efforts in light of what *we* like to do. While we are naturally drawn to our own interests, such an approach can inhibit the work of God and what He wants to do in us and through us. Moreover, our preconceived ideas of what people need can lead us to implement a project that is not a local priority. Remember Jesus and Bartimaeus? Jesus asked, "What do you want me to do for you?" For us to ask that question could be scary because we do not know how God will lead. Who knows what He might ask of us?

Conclusion

God bless you on your mercy-oriented missions efforts as you seek Him and go where He leads. Whether across the street or around the world, may your ministry projects be more than just ministry, and may your efforts intentionally bring people to Jesus and bring glory to God.

So do you want to dig a well in Africa? In the end, the answer seems pretty simple.

- If it helps people,
- if it gives you access to those who have never heard the gospel,
- if it empowers the local church to be on mission with God,
- if it leads to intentional gospel proclamation, *and*
- if the people really want and need a well,

then by all means dig! But dig a well not only for the good of people but also for the glory of God!

Appendix: Next Steps and Resources

Several years ago, a friend who served as a medical missionary in South Asia for several decades shared with me an insight regarding transferring of knowledge to another person. She said to always make it "simple and obvious."

In that spirit, here are some practical next steps for you and your church in relation to your mercy-oriented mission efforts. Whether you are experienced and have done several short-term mission trips with a mercy-oriented component or you are the missions pastor of a church or sending organization, I trust and pray that the following steps and resources will prove useful.

Five Next Steps You Can Take

1. Assess. Conduct an honest assessment of your missions approach and the ministry projects you are involved in. Include those projects in your backyard and around the world. Are they helpful to people in need? Do they facilitate the growth of abilities and capacities of the target group, or do they foster dependency on you? Are the ministries you call "missions" *actually* missions, or are they good ministry projects? Do the projects help people *and* make Christ known?

2. Learn. Discover how others are ensuring an effective and strategic impact in their mercy-oriented missions efforts. There are several good books and resources available

regarding this topic, a few of which are listed at the end of this appendix. Also, other churches, groups, mission pastors, and networks can help you evaluate your mercy-oriented missions projects.

3. Find training. Lots of organization offer training in healthy mercy-oriented missions strategies, practices, and programs. Look at the information and training courses they offer. Also, look to churches and mission organizations doing a good job in mercy-oriented missions and see if they offer training and equipping opportunities.

4. Seek viable partnerships. Work with individuals and organization that implement successful mercy-oriented missions and ask them to mentor you.

5. Pray. Seek God's wisdom in determining what step you need to take next. Who do you need to take that step with? How will you persuade fellow church members to take that step?

A Resource for You to Pursue

Community Development for Kingdom Impact by Jeff Palmer. As a missionary on the field for over twenty years, I learned (the hard way!) how to build a relationship with a community through community development. This book is a culmination of what I have learned. It explains how outsiders can work alongside a community to bring about systemic change but also use that access to gain permission and credibility to share the gospel. It covers topics like the following:

- What is community development?
- How do we enter a community, implement a project, and exit the community?
- Tools for development and interaction with the community.
- Keeping a kingdom-focused community development.

If you are currently involved in or want to be involved in mercy-oriented mission projects, I encourage you and your church to discover and use these tools that will enable you to dialogue with, learn from, and understand local communities from their perspective and their local knowledge. This book is available on www.amazon.com.

Recommended Reading

B elow is a list of recommended reading if you would like to explore this topic more. Some deal directly with missions. Others focus on good development processes with people and communities from a secular perspective.

Church, Missions, and Development

Bradshaw, Bruce. *Bridging the Gap: Evangelism, Development, and Shalom*. California: MARC Publications, 1993.

Cheyne, John R. *Incarnational Agents: A Guide to Developmental Ministry*. Alabama: New Hope, 1996.

Fielding, Charles. *Preach and Heal: A Biblical Model for Missions*. Virginia: International Mission Board, 2008.

Lupton, Robert D. *Compassion, Justice, and the Christian Life: Rethinking Ministry to the Poor*. Ventura: Regal Books, 2007.

Lupton, Robert D. *Toxic Charity: How Churches and Charities Hurt Those They Help–And How to Reverse it*. New York: HarperOne Publishing, 2011.

Myers, Bryant L. *Walking with the Poor: Principles and Practices of Transformational Development*. New York: Orbis Books, 1999.

O'Gorman, Frances. *Charity and Change: From Band-Aid to Beacon.* Australia: World Vision, 1992.

Palmer, J. Jeffrey. *Community Development for Kingdom Impact: Helping People from Here to Eternity.* Nashville: Baptist Global Response, 2016.

Stearns, Richard. *The Hole in Our Gospel.* Nashville: Thomas Nelson Publishers, 2009.

Christians and Hunger Issues

Brown, Lester R. *Tough Choices: Facing the Challenge of Food Scarcity.* The World Watch Environment Alert Series. New York: W. W. Norton Company, 1996.

Parham, Robert. *What Shall We Do in a Hungry World?* Birmingham: New Hope Publications, 1988.

Sider, Ronald J. *Rich Christians in an Age of Hunger: Moving from Affluence to Generosity.* Nashville: W. Publishing Group, 2015.

General Development and Participatory Methods

Bunch, Roland. *Two Ears of Corn: A Guide to People-Centered Agricultural Improvement.* Oklahoma City: World Neighbors, 1985.

Chambers, Robert. *Whose Reality Counts: Putting the First Last.* London: ITDG Publishing, 1997.

Diamond, Jared. *Collapse: How Societies Choose to Fail or Survive.* Penguin Books: London, 2005.

Diamond, Jared. *Guns, Germs, and Steel: A Short History of Everybody for the Last 13,000 Years.* London: Vintage House Publishing, 1997.

Harrison, Lawrence E. Updated Edition. *Underdevelopment Is a State of Mind: The Latin American Case.* Seattle: Madison Books, 2000.

Shumacher, E. F. *Small Is Beautiful: Economics as if People Mattered.* New York: Harper and Row Publishers, Inc., 1973.

Macro-Development Issues (Global Perspectives)

Acemoglu, Daron, and James A. Robinson. *Why Nations Fail: The Origins of Power, Prosperity, and Poverty.* New York: Crown Publishers, 2012.

Asmus, Barry, and Wayne Grudem. *The Poverty of Nations: A Sustainable Solution.* Illinois: Crossway, 2012.

Collier, Paul. *The Bottom Billion: Why the Poorest Countries Are Failing and What Can Be Done about It.* London: Oxford University Press, 2007.

Collins, Daryl, Jonathan Morduch, Stuart Rutherford, Orlanda Ruthven. *Portfolios of the Poor: How the World's Poor Live on $2 a Day.* Princeton: Princeton University Press, 2009.

Deaton, Angus. *The Great Escape: Health, Wealth, and the Origins of Inequality.* Princeton: Princeton University Press, 2013.

Easterly, William. *The White Man's Burden.* London: Oxford University Press, 2006.

Friedman, Thomas L. *The World Is Flat: A Brief History of the Twenty-First Century.* New York: Farrar, Straus, and Giroux, 2005.

Landes, David. *The Wealth and Poverty of Nations: Why Some Are So Rich and Some Are So Poor.* New York: W. W. Norton and Company, 1999.

Peet, Richard and Elaine Hart. *Theories of Development: Contentions, Arguments, Alternatives.* 3rd Edition. New York/London: The Guilford Press, 2015.

Piketty, Thomas. *Capital in the Twenty-First Century.* London: Belknap Press, 2014.

Rist, Gilbert. *The History of Development: From Western Origins to Global Faith.* 3rd Edition. London: Zed Books, 2002.

Sachs, Jeffrey. *The End of Poverty: How We Can Make It Happen in Our Lifetime.* London: Penguin Books Ltd., 2005.

Sitlitz, Joseph E. *The Price of Inequality: How Today's Divided Society Endangers Our Future.* New York: W. W. Norton Company, 2012.

Smith, Adam, and Edwin Cannan. *An Inquiry into the Nature and Causes of the Wealth of Nations.* London: Methuen, 1922. Print.

Weber, Max. *The Protestant Ethic and the Spirit of Capitalism.* New York: Scribner, 1958. Print.

Author's Page: Get to Know Jeff Better...

Jeff Palmer is passionate about helping people in need and making Christ known. His experiences through the years in cross-cultural, mercy-oriented international mission work have given him a unique perspective on how to help people in need while at the same time bringing about Kingdom impact. Jeff is willing to share his experiences, both positive and negative, to help others who desire to make a difference in people's lives both here on earth and for eternity.

Most of what Jeff has learned and shares is based upon his background in rural agriculture, his practical experiences in overseas mission work, and his knowledge gleaned through years of working with the poor and those with limited gospel access. However, the principles and lessons Jeff teaches is applicable to the church and local mission work in the USA as well.

Some of the services offered by Jeff include:

- Additional books and articles on poverty, community development, and the gospel
- Training in community development strategies and missions
- Availability as an event or missions conference speaker
- Consultancy to help you or your group find better ways to address human needs and ensure gospel impact

If you would like to contact Jeff for further information and tap into the many resources that he can provide, connect with him through one of the following ways:

Jeff's Website: www.jonjeffreypalmer.com
Email: jjeffreypalmer@gmail.com
Facebook: www.facebook.com/jeff.palmer.1806
Twitter: @jjeffreypalmer

Printed in the United States
By Bookmasters